Natural Born Fillers

Natural Born Fillers

high energy · fast food · naturally healthy

Silvana Franco

CASSELL
ILLUSTRATED

First published in Great Britain in 2006 by Cassell Illustrated,
a division of Octopus Publishing Group Limited, 2-4 Heron Quays, London E14 4JP

Distributed in the United States of America by
Sterling Publishing Co., Inc., 387 Park Avenue South, New York, NY 10016-8810

A CIP catalogue record for this book is available from the British Library.

ISBN-13: 978-1-844034-41-3
ISBN-10: 1-844034-41-0

10 9 8 7 6 5 4 3 2 1

Photography by Craig Robertson
Design by John Round
Editor Barbara Dixon
Art Director Auberon Hedgecoe
Publishing Manager Anna Cheifetz
Printed in China

Contents

Introduction

So, Natural Born Fillers – natural, organic produce used to make delicious, sustaining recipes to fill any gap. This book is a selection of my most favourite everyday dishes. It's about making the way you cook and eat fit into the way you choose to live your life. Simple, tasty food that everyone can cook and enjoy and it just happens to be good for you too. Fruity porridge, freshly blended juices, wholesome soups, giant salads and scrumptious puddings such as Buttermilk baked custard – you and your family will love these dishes and they will love you right back!

Be healthy

We are all used to hearing that 'you are what you eat' and most of us accept that this is true. If you feed your body the best possible source of fuel then it will thrive.

What you eat is the key to how you feel. Choose natural and wholesome, choose fruit and vegetables, brown before white and where possible unrefined. Add the odd treat once in a while, a fruity pudding, maybe a square of dark chocolate or the odd glass of wine if you want it and you will find you are eating a healthy, balanced diet and feeling great. Most importantly of all you will be choosing to eat food that you enjoy. Unrefined, natural food really does taste best.

Organic

I strongly recommend buying organic wherever possible. When it comes to fresh fruit and vegetables it is especially important if you plan to eat the skin – as for baked potatoes, juicing and ready-to-eat fresh fruit. All non-organic fresh fruit and vegetables must be

peeled before use. There are many reasons why I fly the organic flag but here are my top five:

1. Pesticides, herbicides and a host of other chemicals routinely sprayed on conventionally grown fruit and vegetables can seriously damage your health.
2. Fresh organic produce on average contains one and a half times the vitamins, minerals, enzymes and other nutrients of non-organic goods.
3. Organic animals are not treated with antibiotics, hormones and other medicines systematically used on intensively-reared animals. Nor are they fed GM foods.
4. Organic produce on the whole, tastes much better.
5. Organic food is now more widely available and the price difference is lowering all the time.

So, there's no excuse for skimping. Choose organic meat and free-range eggs and try subscribing to a regular fruit and vegetable box scheme. Most of the schemes operate in the same way by offering a range of different-sized boxes containing a selection of seasonal produce. The produce normally goes from the supplier straight to the distributor cutting out the shop in between so you may be surprised to find it's not as expensive as you might expect. Occasionally, you can find yourself with a surplus of something or other but remember, if you can't juice it, you can almost certainly make a soup out of it! So, all that remains is to get down to the cooking...

Silvana

Breakfast on the go

Creamy ricotta omelette on toast

This recipe is by my chum, food writer Angela Boggiano who has taken her inspiration from the Spanish classic tortilla. Her addition of ricotta and mint gives the omelette a fantastic flavour and texture. Perfect for a laid-back breakfast or lunch – and you can even switch the mint for pancetta if you prefer.

1 Preheat the grill to medium. Drop the new potatoes into a small saucepan and cover with water. Bring to the boil and simmer for 15 minutes until tender. Drain and leave to cool slightly, then slice thinly.

2 Heat the oil in a large frying pan with a heat-proof handle and cook the spring onions for just a minute then add the potatoes, peas and broad beans to the pan.

3 Mix the mint into the beaten eggs along with some salt and pepper then pour over the vegetables in the pan. Dollop tablespoons of ricotta on top and cook gently over a medium heat until the base of the omelette is set and golden. Sprinkle the crumbled Parmesan on top.

4 Meanwhile toast the bread under the grill and then place on serving plates.

5 Place the omelette under the grill and cook until golden and just set. Slice into wedges and serve on the toasts sprinkled with salad cress and plenty of ground black pepper.

Serves 2

200 g/7 oz small new potatoes

1 tablespoon extra virgin olive oil

1 bunch spring onions, chopped

50 g/2 oz frozen peas

50 g/2 oz broad beans

3 tablespoons chopped fresh mint

4 eggs, beaten

100 g/ 3½ oz ricotta cheese

small piece of Parmesan cheese, crumbled

4 slices crusty Granary bread or sourdough bread

125 g/4 oz pot salad cress

sea salt and freshly ground black pepper

Mapled brown bread clusters

These lovely little nutty clusters are wonderful with milk or yoghurt.

Makes/serves 8

200 g/7 oz brown bread

75 g/3 oz pecans, finely chopped

¼ teaspoon ground cinnamon

75 g/3 oz melted butter

4 tablespoons maple syrup

3 tablespoons light muscovado sugar

1 Preheat the oven to 170°C/325°F/mark 3. Whiz the bread in a food processor to form rough crumbs. Tip into a bowl and stir in the nuts, cinnamon, butter, syrup and sugar.

2 Spread out on a large baking sheet and bake in the oven for 20–25 minutes until golden and crusty. Leave to cool, then break up any large clumps. Store in an airtight container.

Tea-steeped fruit salad

This takes a little bit of preparation the night before, but it will yield enough for breakfast for four days and, honestly, if you eat it for four consecutive days you will feel fantastic.

Serves 4

3 Earl Grey tea bags

750 ml/1¼ pints boiling water

100 g/3½ oz pitted prunes

100 g/3½ oz dried unsulphured apricots

100 g/3½ oz large raisins

50 g/2 oz dried cranberries or blueberries

grated rind and juice of 1 unwaxed orange

natural yoghurt and chopped hazelnuts or almonds, to serve

1 Use the tea bags and boiling water to make tea and leave to stand for 10 minutes.

2 Place all the fruit in a pan, pour in the tea (take out the bags) and bring back to the boil, then remove from the heat and leave to cool.

3 Stir in the orange rind and juice and chill for a few hours before eating.

4 To serve, spoon into bowls and top with the yoghurt and nuts.

Potted fruity porridge

Honey porridge

Such a brilliant summer breakfast! Make it the night before, forget about it, go to bed and you'll be delighted when you get up and find it waiting in the fridge for you. If you're running late, just pop the pot into your bag and eat it when you get to work.

If you're making it just for you, eat one portion warm, then chill the other half and eat it cold the next day. Yum!

Serves 2

50 g/2 oz porridge oats

1 tablespoon wheat bran

200 ml/7 fl oz water

175 ml/6 fl oz whole milk

1 tablespoon golden caster sugar

a pinch of salt

2–4 tablespoons clear honey

Makes 4 small pots

50 g/2 oz porridge oats

350 ml/12 fl oz whole milk

8 dried apricots, chopped

2 tablespoons small sultanas

1–2 tablespoons light muscovado sugar

a pinch of salt

1 ripe peach, halved and stoned

1 Place the oats, milk, apricots, sultanas, sugar and salt in a small pan and gently heat together for 10 minutes.

2 Chop the peach and stir into the porridge and simmer for a further 5 minutes or so until the oats are tender and the mixture is thick and creamy.

3 Spoon into 4 small ramekins or pots and leave to cool, then cover and chill.

1 Place the oats, bran, water, milk, salt and sugar in a small pan and gently heat together for 10–15 minutes until the oats are tender and the mixture is thick and creamy.

2 Spoon into 2 small bowls, drizzle over the honey and serve.

Walnut bran muffins

Honestly, they taste lovely!

1 Preheat the oven to 190°C/375°F/mark 5. Line a 12-hole muffin tin with paper cake cases.

2 Gently warm the buttermilk, just for a minute or 2, taking care not to let it boil. Place the cereal in a large heatproof bowl, pour over the warm buttermilk and set aside for 5 minutes.

3 Mash the bananas and stir into the cereal along with the sugar, egg and butter.

4 Gently fold in the flour and nuts, then spoon the mixture into the paper cake cases in the muffin tin. Push a date into the centre of each muffin then bake in the oven for 20–25 minutes until cooked through and nicely browned.

Makes 12

284 ml/½ pint carton buttermilk

250 g/9 oz All-bran cereal

2 ripe bananas

125 g/4 oz light muscovado sugar

1 egg, beaten

125 g/4 oz butter, melted

350 g/12 oz self-raising flour

100 g/3½ oz chopped walnuts

12 dates

Spiced berry scones

Scones are sturdy enough to survive a bus journey in your pocket so they make a great choice for breakfast on the run. These are flavoursome enough to eat plain or toasted, but are even better split and sandwiched with soft cheese. And they freeze really well, too – make them over the weekend and cool, then pack two at a time into ziplock bags and freeze. Just remember to take a bag out of the freezer before you go to bed so they're ready for the morning!

1   Preheat the oven to 220°C/425°F/mark 7. Place all the flour in a large bowl, then rub in the butter. Using a table knife, stir in the sugar, berries, mixed spice and salt, then add the milk and stir in – if it feels a little dry, add a touch more milk, then bring together to make a soft dough.

2   Lightly dust the surface with a little flour, then roll out the dough no thinner than 2.5 cm/1 inch. Using a 5 cm/2 inch plain cutter, firmly stamp out the rounds – try not to twist the cutter as this makes the scones rise unevenly. Re-roll the trimmings and stamp out more rounds.

3   Transfer the rounds to a non-stick baking sheet and dust with a little more flour, then bake in the oven for 12–15 minutes until well risen and golden. Cool on a wire rack and serve just warm or at room temperature. They only last a day or two, so freeze any you don't eat.

Makes 12

100 g/3½ oz wholemeal flour

150 g/5 oz self-raising flour, plus extra for dusting

50 g/2 oz butter, at room temperature

50 g/2 oz golden caster sugar

75 g/3 oz dried mixed berries or cranberries

½ teaspoon ground mixed spice

a pinch of salt

150 ml/ ¼ pint whole milk

Pumpkin seed and apricot energy bars

Here is my version of those high-energy cereal bars you can buy. These are scrumptious, quite chewy and full of goodness.

1 Stir the sugar into the condensed milk and set aside to dissolve.

2 Preheat the oven to 180°C/350°F/mark 4. In a large bowl, mix the apricots with the oats, seeds, nuts and cereal. Stir in the condensed milk until well blended.

3 Spoon the mixture into a non-stick 12 x 25 cm/5 x 10 inch tin, pressing down to ensure an even surface. Bake in the oven for 20–25 minutes until golden, then remove from the oven and leave to cool in the tin.

4 Turn out of the tin and cut into 16 bars. Wrap each one in a rectangle of waxed or greaseproof paper and store in an airtight container.

Makes 16

1 tablespoon dark muscovado sugar

250 ml/8 fl oz whole condensed milk

175 g/6 oz soft dried unsulphured apricots, roughly chopped

150 g/5 oz porridge oats

50 g/2 oz pumpkin seeds

50 g/2 oz whole almonds, roughly chopped

50 g/2 oz puffed wholegrain rice cereal

Potato and spring onion pancakes

What a weekend treat! Especially when topped with a few waves of smoked salmon, a soft-boiled egg or a couple of crisp rashers of streaky bacon with the rind still on. There are so many interesting flours around now to experiment with. I love these pancakes made with buckwheat flour, but try with other types and see what hits the right note for you.

1 Boil the potatoes until tender, then mash thoroughly – lumps will really spoil the pancakes so it is worth passing them through a ricer or a mouli.

2 Stir in the milk, flour, spring onions and salt to taste and leave to cool for 5 minutes. When the mash is cool enough not to set the eggs, stir in the yolks.

3 In a separate bowl, whisk the egg whites until softly peaking, then fold into the potato mixture.

4 Brush a non-stick frying pan with a little oil and heat until hot. Drop spoonfuls of the batter into the hot pan and cook for a couple of minutes or so on each side until puffed and golden. Serve warm.

Makes 12 pancakes

500 g/1 lb 2 oz white potatoes, peeled and cubed

125 ml/4 fl oz whole milk

50 g/2 oz self-raising flour

1 bunch of spring onions, thinly sliced

3 eggs, separated

sea salt

olive oil, for frying

The morning-after cure

Yes, we know, 'never again'! You feel shocking and think you want a can of cola, but no, actually this is what'll get you back on your feet again and for more than five minutes. It's easy to drink and loaded with vitamins and some natural sugar for instant energy. Follow this with a Spiced berry scone (page 15) or some wholegrain toast and you'll feel as good as new.

Serves 1

4 large carrots, cut into large chunks

2 red apples, cut into wedges

pulp and seeds from 2 passion fruit

Juice the carrots and apples, then stir in the passion fruit pulp and seeds. Drink it all.

Banana prune malt shake

I've never understood why malts aren't as popular as smoothies. Malt tastes wonderful and it's good for your digestion, so along with the prunes and banana this is certainly one to get you going in the morning. You can find malt extract in health food stores, but if you buy it from the chemist avoid the one with cod liver oil added to it – it may be good for you but it doesn't go very well with banana!

Serves 2

2 ripe bananas

8 plump moist pitted prunes

1 tablespoon malt extract

300 ml/½ pint whole milk

Break the bananas into a blender, then add the prunes, malt extract and milk. Whiz until thick and frothy and drink straightaway.

Purple juice zinger

Red cabbage juice might not sound like everyone's ideal start to the day, but this is not only delicious, it's also packed with vitamins and antioxidants. When it comes to juicing it is best to go organic and save yourself the time and energy of peeling the fruit and vegetables first.

Serves 2

1 small red cabbage, cut into large chunks

3 sweet red apples, cut into wedges

1 large knob of fresh root ginger, peeled

Pass the cabbage, apples, and ginger through a juicer. Pour into two glasses, adding a cube or two of ice if you have any, and drink swiftly before the vitamins begin to deteriorate.

Beetroot purifier

Beetroot juice is fantastic – as well as being vitamin and mineral packed, it is very cleansing and can help alleviate many ailments including constipation and bladder, kidney and liver disorders. It is also said to stimulate the metabolism and I promise you, you'll even learn to enjoy the taste. Try to drink this once a week.

Serves 1

1 small raw beetroot

2 pears, quartered

2 celery stalks

1 lime, peeled

Scrub the beetroot, then trim off the end and quarter it lengthways. Pass the beetroot, pears, celery and lime through a juicer and drink swiftly before the vitamins begin to deteriorate.

Pure mango slush

Apple and mango make a perfect combination.

Serves 2
1 large mango, peeled, stoned and diced
100 ml/3½ fl oz pressed fresh apple juice
1 large glass of ice

Place the mango, apple juice and ice in a blender and whiz together until smooth and slushy. Pour into glasses and serve.

Breakfast in a glass (and a half!)

This super smoothie takes a couple of minutes to whiz up, but contains so much goodness it'll keep you going right through to lunch.

Serves 1
250 g/9 oz mixed berries such as strawberries, blueberries and blackberries
1 small knob of fresh root ginger, peeled and chopped
150 ml/¼ pint pressed fresh apple juice
a small handful of porridge oats
150 g/5 oz natural yoghurt
1–2 tablespoons clear honey

1 Place the berries and ginger in a blender and whiz until smooth.

2 Add the apple juice, oats, yoghurt and honey and whiz until frothy. Pour into a very large glass (it makes about 450 ml/¾ pint) and drink.

Little Fillers

Hellfire chicken wings

I just can't write a book without including a recipe for chicken wings as I'm such a fan. Lately though, it seems chicken wings have been downgraded in the supermarket and are mass-packed as an economy product – such a shame, as the wings are surely the most enjoyable part of the chicken, although I admit not the leanest. Nowadays, I buy mine from my local butcher who deals only in organic birds and he charges very little for the wings as they're less popular than they used to be – surprising as they're always the first to disappear from the barbecue or picnic basket!

And if you are a chilli addict like me, don't worry about indulging – it is said to be a tonic for many things including sore throat, blocked sinuses, tummy ache, poor complexion, hangovers and bad circulation. A full tablespoon of cayenne does push the chilli kick quite far, so you may prefer to use 1–2 teaspoons.

Serves 4

grated rind and juice of
1 small unwaxed orange

1 tablespoon dark muscovado sugar

1 tablespoon maple syrup or clear honey

1 tablespoon cayenne

¼ teaspoon sea salt

12 large chicken wings

1 Preheat the oven to 200°C/400°F/mark 6. Place the orange rind and juice in a large bowl and stir in the sugar, syrup or honey, the cayenne and salt.

2 Add the chicken wings and turn them to coat in the mixture. If you have time, leave to marinate for a while; otherwise, place on a rack set over a baking sheet and roast in the oven for 20–25 minutes until golden brown and very hot and sticky.

Roasted butternut and Gorgonzola purée

Squash and pumpkins all roast beautifully, but some do taste better than others. The butternut is very common and has a lovely nutty flavour and silky texture when puréed. As well as being high in fibre, pumpkins are also an excellent source of vitamin A, which is good for our eyes, skin, hair and teeth.

Serves/makes 4

1 large butternut squash

1 tablespoon olive oil

a pinch of ground cumin

50–75 g/2–3 oz Gorgonzola or other strong blue cheese

1 Preheat the oven to 200°C/400°F/mark 6. Halve the squash and scoop out and discard the seeds. Score the flesh deeply in a criss-cross pattern to help it cook evenly, then drizzle with the oil and sprinkle with the cumin. Roast in the oven for 30 minutes or so until the flesh is tender.

2 Scoop the flesh into a bowl and roughly mash. Stir in the cheese and serve just as it's melting.

Green chilli and cumin labneh

Labneh is a traditional Lebanese soft cheese made from sheep or goats' milk. My cheats' version is made from Greek yoghurt and still has a gorgeous twang to it, but by all means try making it with sheep or goats' milk yoghurt, too.

1 Add the salt to the yoghurt and stir together. Place a square of muslin (I use a baby's cloth) or a rinsed new J-cloth in a bowl and spoon in the yoghurt. Gather the ends together and tie firmly with string. Suspend the yoghurt above a sink or deep bowl (I normally tie the string to a wooden spoon and suspend it over a large jug) and leave overnight in a cool room.

2 Next morning, the excess liquid will have dripped out and you will be left with a firm, soft cheese in the cloth. Transfer the cheese to a bowl and stir in the chilli and cumin seeds. Drizzle the surface with the oil and chill until ready to eat. It will keep in the fridge for up to three days. Serve with pitta or breadsticks.

Serves 6

½ teaspoon sea salt

500 g/1 lb 2 oz Greek yoghurt

1 green chilli, deseeded and finely chopped

1 teaspoon toasted cumin seeds

1 teaspoon extra virgin olive oil

warm pitta or breadsticks, to serve

Pecorino croutons

Pecorino is a Parmesan-style cheese made from sheeps' milk. Like Parmesan, it can be used at varying levels of maturity, but mostly in the UK we get it when it's quite hard and mature and good for grating. When I was a kid, my mum used to age huge wheels of it on a specially built shelf in the shed at home and used it so heavy-handedly in her cooking that it is only in recent years that I have finally learnt to love it.

I use a flavoured focaccia, such as one with rosemary or olives in it, for this recipe as the texture and olive oil content makes for a good crunchy result. Great for dipping!

1 Preheat the oven to 200°C/400°F/mark 6. Place the focaccia in a large bowl. Sprinkle over the pecorino and toss well together. The focaccia should have enough oil in it to make the cheese stick, but if not add a little splash of oil.

2 Scatter the focaccia cubes onto a large non-stick baking sheet in a single layer. Bake in the oven for 12 minutes until crunchy and golden. Leave to cool and store in an airtight tin.

Makes/serves 6

400 g/14 oz flavoured focaccia loaf, cut into cubes

a large handful of fresh, finely grated pecorino cheese

olive oil

Skordalia

Skordalia is a Greek garlic and olive oil dip/side dish that is especially good with white fish and can be made in a variety of different ways. Unlike hummus and taramasalata, skordalia is rarely seen outside of restaurants, which is a shame. This recipe is potato-based, but it can be bread-based, too – Jane Grigson's version from her wonderful *Fish Book* is a gorgeous-textured, garlic mayonnaise thickened with breadcrumbs and almonds.

Don't make this with a red-skinned or waxy new potato as you won't get a good result. Choose a floury, white-skinned variety such as Maris Piper.

Serves 4–6

500 g/1 lb 2 oz white floury potatoes, peeled and cubed

4 plump garlic cloves, peeled and quartered

2 tablespoons white wine vinegar

150 ml/¼ pint extra virgin olive oil

sea salt

1 Cook the potatoes in a pan of boiling water until tender.

2 Place the garlic in a food processor with a big pinch of salt and whiz until finely chopped. Drain the potatoes well, then add to the processor with the vinegar and whiz until very smooth. Now, slowly pour in the oil to make a glossy dip. Delicious!

lemon mozzarella crostini

Choose good bread, top-quality mozzarella and keep this simple.

1 Drain the mozzarella and tear into pieces. Pop into a bowl with 1 tablespoon of the oil, the lemon rind and juice and basil and stir well together.

2 Preheat a griddle pan. Cut each slice of bread into quarters and drizzle over a little olive oil. Cook in the hot pan for a minute or so on each side until brown and a little charred.

3 Rub each piece of toast with the cut surface of the garlic clove and season with a little salt. Top with the mozzarella and serve while the toast is still warm.

Serves 2

125–150 g/4–5 oz ball buffalo mozzarella

2 tablespoons extra virgin olive oil or avocado oil

grated rind and juice of 1 small unwaxed lemon

a few torn fresh basil leaves

2 slices of sourdough bread

1 unpeeled garlic clove, halved

sea salt

Mr Ganoush's baba ganoush

Aubergines are my favourite vegetable and this has to be one of my favourite ways of using them. So keen am I on this dish, that Baba Ganoush is, in fact, my little son's nickname ('Mr Ganoush' when he's in trouble). To be honest, he's not always very keen on eating the classic version, but this one is softened with a spoonful of Greek yoghurt and is very child-friendly. Serve with strips of warm flat bread or pitta, for dipping.

1 Preheat the oven to 200°C/400°F/mark 6. Pop the aubergines onto a baking sheet and roast in the oven for 20–25 minutes until wrinkled and softened.

2 Split the aubergines open (be careful of the steam) and scoop the flesh into a food processor along with the garlic, cumin and yoghurt. Whiz until smooth.

3 Stir in the mint, then add the citrus juice and salt, to taste. Will keep in the fridge for 2–3 days.

Serves 4–6

2 aubergines

1 garlic clove, peeled and crushed

1 teaspoon ground cumin

2–3 tablespoons Greek yoghurt

2 tablespoons finely chopped fresh mint

a squeeze of fresh lemon or lime juice

sea salt

Soft butterbean pâté

Butterbeans are very under-used, if you ask me. They have such a lovely soft texture when puréed, which makes them great for pâtés and spreads. Warmed, mashed butterbeans, perhaps with a little cheese melted in, make a great alternative to mashed potatoes.

1 Place the beans in a food processor and whiz to break them down. The mixture will be stiff so add the oil and 3–4 table-spoons of water until you get a nice smooth texture.

2 Stir in the chives and chilli and add lemon juice and salt and pepper to taste. Spoon into a bowl, drizzle over a little oil and chill until ready to serve. Will keep in the fridge for 2–3 days.

Serves 4–6

2 x 410 g/14½ oz cans butterbeans, drained and rinsed

3 tablespoons extra virgin olive oil, plus extra for drizzling

3 tablespoons chopped fresh chives

1 fresh chilli, deseeded and finely chopped

juice of ½ lemon

sea salt and freshly ground black pepper

Red pepper pesto

This is a very useful little sauce – great for spreading on bruschetta, dipping grissini or croutons into (try with Pecorino croutons on page 30) or tossing with hot pasta.

1 Cook the red peppers under a hot grill for 15–20 minutes until blackened and blistered all over. Place in a bowl and cover with a tea towel – the steam will soften the skin and make them easier to peel.

2 Scatter the nuts on a baking sheet. Lower the heat of the grill to medium and toast them for a few minutes until golden brown. Leave to cool a little, while you peel and deseed the peppers.

3 Place the skinned peppers, almonds and garlic in a food processor and whiz until as smooth as possible. Mix in the chilli flakes, vinegar and oil and season generously. Cover and chill for up to 2 days.

Serves 4
2 large red peppers

50 g/2 oz blanched almonds

1 garlic clove, peeled

a large pinch of crushed chilli flakes

1 teaspoon balsamic vinegar

2 tablespoons extra virgin olive oil

sea salt and freshly ground black pepper

Simple smoked mackerel spread

Mackerel is the kind of oily fish we should all be eating at least twice a week. It's loaded with heart-friendly omega oils and the smoked varieties are easy to turn into delicious spreads. Good for salads and sandwiches.

Serves 4–6

275 g/10 oz smoked mackerel fillets

125 g/4 oz soft cheese

a few shakes of Tabasco or other chilli sauce

a squeeze of fresh lemon or lime juice

2 spring onions, chopped

freshly ground black pepper

1   Skin the mackerel fillets and lift out and discard the dark flesh that runs down the back of each fillet – this is the blood line and can taste bitter.

2   Break the fish into a bowl, add the soft cheese and, using a fork, mash together. Add the chilli, citrus juice and spring onions and season with black pepper. Cover and chill for up to 3 days.

Beetroot hummus

Couldn't be easier (or packed with many more vitamins, fibre and antioxidants)!

Serves 4

2 cooked vacuum-packed beetroot

400 g/14 oz can chickpeas, drained

1 shallot, peeled and finely chopped

3 tablespoons chopped fresh parsley

1 small garlic clove, peeled and crushed

1 tablespoon wine vinegar

2 tablespoons olive oil

sea salt and freshly ground black pepper

1   Put the beetroot and chickpeas in a food processor and whiz until as smooth as possible.

2   Stir in the shallot, parsley, garlic, vinegar and oil and season to taste. Chill until ready to eat. Will keep in the fridge for up to 2 days.

Potted Cheshire

Cheese is often thought of as unhealthy, but it is a very valuable source of calcium. These little pots are brilliant for parties and picnics. Vary the quantities depending on how much cheese you've got to use up – any crumbly cheese such as Caerphilly or Wensleydale will do fine. For a French-style potted cheese, skip the pepper sauce and add a splash of brandy instead. Serve with some Granary toast.

Serves 4

150 g/5 oz Cheshire cheese, crumbled

50 g/2 oz soft cheese

25 g/1 oz unsalted butter

a few shakes of Tabasco

Whiz all the ingredients together in a food processor until well blended but still slightly textured. Spoon into small pots or ramekins and smooth the tops. Cover with plastic wrap and chill until ready to serve. Will keep in the fridge for up to 4 days.

Paprika'd popcorn

It's such a shame we associate popcorn only with going to the flicks, when it is so easy to make at home. Popcorn is a nutritious snack that gets a bad reputation from being smothered in butter and sugar. A little oil, a bit of spice and in a matter of minutes you've got a delicious snack that is healthier and tastier than any packet of crisps.

Serves 1–2

25 g/1 oz popping corn

1 teaspoon vegetable oil

1 teaspoon paprika

sea salt

1 Place the corn and oil in a large pan, cover with a lid and set over a medium-high heat. Cook for 5 minutes or so until all the popping subsides.

2 Add the paprika and some sea salt and shake the pan vigorously. Best served warm, but any leftovers can be stored for a few days in an airtight container.

Avocado and basil mayo

Did you know the avocado is listed in *The Guinness Book of Records* as the most nutritious fruit known to man? Not only is it packed with vitamins, fibre and heart-friendly oils, the taste and texture of the avocado is just fantastic. This dip is leaning towards guacamole, but the texture is creamy and smooth like that of mayonnaise. The avocados you choose must be ripe, and I sometimes stir in a very finely chopped shallot at the last minute.

1 Place the garlic, basil and some salt in a mini food processor and whiz until blended to a paste.

2 Add the avocados and whiz until smooth. Blend in the oil and vinegar and check the seasoning. It discolours fairly quickly so don't make this too far ahead of time. Serve at room temperature.

Serves 4–6

1 garlic clove, peeled and crushed

a large handful of fresh basil leaves

2 ripe avocados, halved, skinned, stoned and cubed

2 tablespoons avocado oil or extra virgin olive oil

2 teaspoons wine vinegar

sea salt and freshly ground black pepper

Home-spiced tortilla chips

These are very easy to make and you can vary the heat factor depending on what mood you're in. Serve with a simple tomato salsa (see below) for dipping.

1 Mix the oil with the spices and brush over the tortillas. Cut each one into 16 wedges – slice them as though you were cutting a cake.

2 Place the wedges in a single layer on a large baking sheet. Cook under a medium grill for 4–5 minutes until crisp and golden brown and maybe a touch charred at the tips. Serve warm or at room temperature.

Simple tomato salsa
Roughly chop 1 garlic clove and 1 shallot or a spring onion or two. Whiz in a mini food processor until finely minced, then add 2 roughly chopped ripe tomatoes and a splash of olive oil and whiz again. Add salt, a squeeze of lemon juice and any chopped herbs you have to hand.

Serves 2
1 tablespoon olive or vegetable oil
¼ teaspoon cayenne
¼ teaspoon ground cumin
¼ teaspoon ground coriander
2 soft corn tortillas

Sandwiches, wraps and toasties

Red Leicester nonsense with dill pickle

I quite like Quark – it's very neutral, which means it's excellent for binding things together without interfering with their flavour too much. It is naturally low in fat and is readily available in most supermarkets. In Germany the work 'quark' is used conversationally to mean 'nonsense!'.

1 Bring a small pan of water to the boil, add the eggs and boil for 8 minutes, then drain them and cool under water.

2 Shell the eggs, then mash them with a fork. Stir in the cheeses, onion and plenty of black pepper.

3 Spread some of the filling onto two slices of the bread, then lay on the sliced pickles. Top with the rest of the filling, then sandwich with the remaining two slices of bread. Squash down a bit, then cut and eat.

Serves 2

2 large eggs, at room temperature

75 g/3 oz good-quality Red Leicester cheese, coarsely grated

75 g/3 oz Quark or other soft cheese

1 small red onion, peeled and finely chopped

4 slices of thickly sliced wholemeal bread, lightly buttered

2 large dill pickles, thinly sliced lengthways

freshly ground black pepper

Crab and crispy bacon doubles

A lovely old-fashioned double decker, this is sort of an updated club sandwich. Make sure you use good quality streaky bacon for a firm, crispy bite.

1 Heat a large non-stick pan and add the bacon. Cook over a high heat for 3–4 minutes until the bacon begins to release its oils into the pan, then add the tomatoes and cook for a further 5 minutes until the bacon is crispy and the tomatoes have softened.

2 Meanwhile, mix the crab with the butter, shallot and cayenne, then add the lime juice and salt and pepper to taste.

3 Make two double-decker sandwiches using the lettuce leaves, crispy bacon and tomatoes on the bottom level and the spiced crab on the top deck. Eat warm or wrap in greaseproof paper and pack into a lunch box.

Serves 2

8 rashers streaky bacon

6 cherry tomatoes, halved

175 g/6 oz can white crab meat, drained

2 tablespoons melted butter

1 shallot, peeled and finely chopped

a pinch of cayenne

a squeeze of fresh lime juice

6 slices of soft Granary bread, lightly buttered

a large handful of baby lettuce leaves

sea salt and freshly ground black pepper

James's Moroccan chicken wrap

This recipe has been devised by my friend James Fisher. He's a very accomplished chef, so this sandwich is a bit more complicated than most of the others in this chapter, but is definitely worth taking the extra time over.

　Although there seems to be lots of fiddly bits and pieces, they all come together fantastically. For the chicken you can use leftovers from a Sunday roast or you can buy thigh and drumstick packs from most supermarkets – just roast them following the instructions on the pack.

1 Preheat the oven to 160°C/325°F/mark 3. Slice the tomatoes in half and place cut-side up on a wire rack set on a baking tray. Sprinkle over the garlic and some black pepper and drizzle over some of the oil. Slow-cook in the oven for 1–2 hours or until the tomatoes have become wrinkled and are beginning to brown. You can make these the day before.

2 Place the chickpeas in a mixing bowl with the parsley, lemon juice, onion, a splash of olive oil, the cumin and some salt and pepper and gently spoon together.

3 Vigorously mix the harissa into the mayo until it is an even pink blush colour.

4 Cook the tortillas in a hot non-stick frying pan for 15 seconds until they begin to blister.

5 To assemble, lay the tortillas on a board. Divide the chicken between them, then top with the chickpea salad, followed by the roasted tomatoes and, finally, spoon over the harissa mayo. Roll up and eat.

Serves 4

4 ripe tomatoes

1 garlic clove, peeled and thinly sliced

2 tablespoons olive oil

400 g/14 oz can chickpeas, drained

1 small bunch of fresh parsley, roughly chopped

juice of 1 lemon

1 red onion, peeled and thinly sliced

½ teaspoon ground cumin

1 teaspoon harissa paste

4 tablespoons mayonnaise

4 flour tortillas

400 g/14 oz roasted chicken, shredded

sea salt and freshly ground black pepper

Wasabi beef and cucumber rolls

This is a very good sandwich if you're not feeling too perky or are suffering the effects of a big night out – the flavours are very lively, it's not too heavy on the carbs and the wasabi is a real head-clearer.

I like to make these using the sort of pancakes you normally use with crispy Peking duck. In the supermarket they are usually stocked in the fridge near the duck. You can use flour tortillas, but they are rather bready.

1 Place the steak in a shallow dish and rub in the soy sauce and sake or sherry. Leave to marinate for 10 minutes to 2 hours.

2 Preheat a griddle pan. Scatter the sugar over the steak, pressing it in with your fingertips and, once the pan is really hot, cook for a couple of minutes on each side until nicely browned but still a little pink in the centre.

3 Leave the steak to rest for 5 minutes, then cut into 1 cm/½ inch thick strips. If you're going to eat the rolls immediately use the steak while still warm, otherwise, leave it to cool completely before rolling.

4 Smear the pancakes or tortillas with wasabi and then roll up with the cucumber, rocket and steak.

Serves 2

1 large trimmed sirloin or rump steak, about 250 g/9 oz

1 tablespoon soy sauce

1 tablespoon sake or dry sherry

1 tablespoon light muscovado or other brown sugar

4 pancakes or 2 flour tortillas

1–2 teaspoons wasabi paste

6 cm/2½ inch piece of cucumber, sliced or cut into matchsticks

a bowl of fresh rocket

Ham on rye with mustard and watercress

Dark rye bread can be a bit overwhelming, so go for a light rye that contains a mix of white and rye flours and ideally some rye seeds, too. The flavour combination of rye, ham and mustard is a long-time classic.

Serves 2

1 tablespoon clear honey

1 tablespoon wholegrain mustard

2 thick slices of baked ham

4 slices of lightly buttered rye bread

a handful of watercress

a few shakes of balsamic vinegar

1 Mix the honey with the mustard.

2 Place the ham on two slices of bread, then top with the watercress. Drizzle over the honey and mustard and splash over a little balsamic vinegar. Sandwich with the remaining slices of bread.

Smoked salmon and salsa verde bagels

A mini-chopper makes very light work of this salsa verde, which will keep in the fridge for a few days and is also good with most cheese and cold meats.

Serves 4

1 spring onion, roughly chopped

1 large gherkin, roughly chopped

2 teaspoons capers, rinsed

1 large bunch of fresh parsley

1 small bunch of fresh mint or coriander

4 tablespoons olive oil

juice of 1 lemon

4 wholegrain bagels

200 g/7 oz smoked salmon

sea salt and freshly ground black pepper

1 Place the spring onion, gherkin, capers, parsley and mint or coriander in a food processor and whiz until chopped and well blended. Add the oil and lemon juice, some salt and black pepper and whiz again to make a coarse paste.

2 Split each bagel and lightly toast the cut sides. Fold the salmon slices over the bases, spoon over the salsa verde and top with the bagel halves.

Great gravlax sandwich

Soft cheese and boiled eggs make perfect companions to cured and smoked fish, cutting through the salty flavour and oily texture perfectly. Given the choice, I go down the Scandinavian route and choose a light rye bread for this sandwich, but if you can't get it, Granary is okay, too. If you want to carry on with the Scandinavian theme, serve this as an open sandwich, smorgasbord style.

1 Bring a small pan of water to the boil, add the eggs and boil for 8 minutes, then drain them and cool under water.

2 Slice the cucumber and place in a bowl with the lemon juice or vinegar and the herbs, separating the slices so the liquid and herbs mingle.

3 Spread the cheese onto two of the slices of bread and top with the gravlax or smoked salmon. Shell and slice the eggs and arrange on top of the fish along with the cucumber, then grind over some pepper.

4 For a closed sandwich, lightly butter the remaining two slices of bread and press down on top, otherwise serve open.

Serves 2

2 large eggs, at room temperature

¼ cucumber

juice of ½ lemon or 1 tablespoon wine vinegar

1–2 tablespoons fresh dill leaves or shredded fresh basil leaves

100 g/3½ oz soft cheese

2 or 4 slices of bread

125 g/4 oz pack gravlax or smoked salmon

a small knob of butter, at room temperature (optional)

freshly ground black pepper

Tuna cobs

In my home town of Derby we call crusty round bread rolls 'cobs', because of their resemblance to the street cobbles. Everywhere else though, they just seem to be called crusty bread rolls, which is not quite as descriptive. Anyway, tuna is a classic filler, but really needs to be paired with something that has a bit of bite and maybe a touch of sweetness – in this case we're using apple. This is a very useful filling and is also great in baked potatoes and pancakes.

1 Quarter, core and chop the apple, but leave the skin on. Mix with the tuna, spring onions, yoghurt, seeds, a squeeze of fresh lime juice and some salt and plenty of black pepper.

2 Split and fill the cobs, wrap in greaseproof paper and pack into a lunch box.

Serves 2

1 red apple

200 g/7 oz can tuna fillets in spring water, drained

4 spring onions, sliced

4 tablespoons Greek yoghurt

1 teaspoon onion seeds or sesame seeds

a squeeze of fresh lime juice

2 cobs

sea salt and freshly ground black pepper

Gruyère and balsamic onion toasties

Most supermarkets stock those jars of gorgeous marinated baby onions and they are just wonderful with cheese. They are, however, pretty pricey and it's easy to make your own balsamic onions at home – I guess it just depends on what you've got in the cupboard and how much time you have.

1 Spread one side of each slice of bread with butter. Divide the cheese and onions between two unbuttered sides and top with the remaining bread, unbuttered side down.

2 Place the sandwiches in a large non-stick frying pan. Turn on the heat – it's a good idea to start heating slowly, otherwise the bread will crisp up before the cheese gets a chance to melt.

3 Cook for a few minutes on each side until the cheese is bubbling around the edges and the bread is crisp and golden. Slide each sandwich onto a plate, cut in half and eat while still warm.

Balsamic onions
Heat 1 spoonful of olive or vegetable oil in a small frying pan and cook 1 sliced onion for a few minutes until beginning to soften and turn golden. If you have any yellow mustard seeds, sprinkle in a few. Now add 1 teaspoon caster sugar and 1 tablespoon balsamic vinegar and cook very gently for a further 5 minutes. If you have any herbs, such as thyme, rosemary or parsley, chop them, add to the onions and cook for a minute or two more. Season with sea salt and freshly ground black pepper.

Serves 2

4 slices of mixed grain country bread

a knob of butter

100 g/3½ oz Gruyère or Emmenthal cheese, thinly sliced or grated

balsamic onions (see below) or 4 marinated onions from a jar, sliced

Avocado and havarti toasted tortillas

Havarti is a lovely buttery-tasting, semi-hard cheese that melts brilliantly. I wouldn't normally pair avocado with cheese and certainly not a Danish one, but it just works so well here.

1 Scoop the avocado out of its shell and cube the flesh. Using a fork, flatten the avocado onto one of the tortillas. Scatter over the cheese and basil and then add some chilli sauce and lime juice and a few good grinds of black pepper.

2 Sandwich the other tortilla on top, then place in a large non-stick frying pan. Turn on the heat – it's a good idea to start heating slowly, otherwise the tortilla will crisp up before the cheese gets a chance to melt.

3 Cook for a few minutes on each side until the cheese is bubbling around the edges and the bread is crisp and golden. Slide the tortilla onto a plate, cut into wedges and eat while still warm.

Serves 1

1 small or ½ avocado

2 flour tortillas

40 g/1½ oz havarti cheese, diced

a few fresh basil leaves

a few shakes of Tabasco or other chilli sauce

a squeeze of fresh lime juice

freshly ground black pepper

Rice paper prawn and glass noodle rolls

These delicate little rolls do take a bit of patience to assemble, but they're great for a special occasion or if you fancy showing off your packed lunch at work. Glass or cellophane noodles are usually made from bean starch and when reconstituted are clear, but vermicelli rice noodles, which are not translucent, make a good substitute and are readily available in supermarkets. Make sure you get all the ingredients prepared before you begin to roll.

1 Place the noodles in a large heatproof bowl, cover with a kettleful of boiling water and set aside for a few minutes until softened, then drain and cool.

2 Fill a large heatproof bowl with hot water. Submerge one rice paper wrapper in the water and soak it for about 1 minute until softened. Carefully remove the rice paper from the water and lay it flat on a clean towel.

3 Place a few noodles, 2 prawns and a sprinkling of spring onions, ginger, sesame seeds and coriander leaves horizontally across the centre of the wrapper. Fold over the left and right edges of the wrapper to enclose the ends of the filling and then, starting at the bottom, roll up to enclose the filling and form a neat cylinder. Repeat to use up all the wrappers and the filling. You may need to replace the hot water if it cools down too much. Chill the rolls, join-side down, until ready to eat.

Dipping sauce
These rolls are often accompanied by a dipping sauce. Mix your own blend or mix 2 tablespoons light soy sauce with 1 tablespoon water, 1 teaspoon rice or wine vinegar and ½ teaspoon Oriental chilli oil.

Serves 4

50 g/2 oz glass or vermicelli rice noodles

16 x 23 cm/9 inch round rice paper wrappers

250 g/9 oz cooked peeled tiger prawns (you'll need 32 in total)

6 spring onions, shredded

1 tablespoon chopped pickled ginger

2 teaspoons sesame seeds

a handful of fresh coriander leaves

dipping sauce, to serve (see below)

Spiced chicken chapattis

I'm cooking the chicken from fresh, but if you're in a hurry you can use marinated cooked chicken fillets from the supermarket. Chapattis are a good alternative to flour tortillas as they tend to be made using a good proportion of wholemeal flour.

1 Preheat the grill to medium. In a shallow bowl, mix half the yoghurt with the curry paste, seeds and some salt and pepper. Dip the chicken in the yoghurt mixture to coat it completely. Grill for 6–8 minutes on each side until nicely browned and cooked through. Leave to cool.

2 Meanwhile, place the garlic, mint and remaining yoghurt in a mini food processor and whiz until the mint is finely chopped in – or you can use a hand-held blender. Add a squeeze of one of the lemon wedges and salt and pepper to taste.

3 Pile the lettuce onto the chapattis. Slice the chicken and arrange on top, then drizzle over the minty yoghurt. Fold in half or roll up and eat.

Serves 2

150 g/5 oz natural yoghurt

1 tablespoon curry paste

¼ teaspoon mustard seeds

¼ teaspoon cumin seeds

2 small skinless boneless chicken breasts

1 small garlic clove, peeled

1 bunch of fresh mint

1 lemon, cut into wedges

1 little gem lettuce, shredded

2 chapattis

sea salt and freshly ground black pepper

Simple salad sandwich

I don't know about you, but sometimes I just want a simple salad sandwich. This is the best one I know.

1 Mix the carrot with the spring onion, linseeds, a good squeeze of lemon juice and some salt and pepper.

2 Arrange the spinach or rocket leaves and the tomato on one slice of the bread, then pile on the carrot mixture. Scatter the sprouts on top, sandwich with the remaining slice and serve.

Serves 1

1 carrot, peeled and coarsely grated

1 spring onion, shredded

1 teaspoon linseeds

a squeeze of fresh lemon juice

a large handful of baby spinach or rocket leaves

1 firm tomato, sliced

2 slices of Granary bread, lightly spread with mayonnaise

a large handful of mustard and cress or alfalfa sprouts

sea salt and freshly ground black pepper

Real falafel with flat breads

Some of you may argue that falafel are actually deep-fried fast food and there is a point to that argument because, yes, they are indeed fried. But, they taste so wonderful I could never give them up. And they are made almost entirely of chickpeas, which contain phytochemicals called saponins, which act as antioxidants. They can help to lower cholesterol levels and are also a good source of protein and fibre. And this is the only deep-fried recipe in the book!

Real falafel are made using dried chickpeas, which have to be soaked overnight and so makes them appear time consuming, but really they're so simple – just put the chickpeas in to soak before you go to bed.

1 To make the falafel, place all the ingredients except the sunflower oil in a food processor and whiz to a rough purée.

2 Using your hands, very firmly shape the mixture into 30 balls, then pat each one into a little cake. If the mixture starts to stick, dampen your hands with water. Be firm or the cakes may break during frying. If you have time now, chill them for a while.

3 Heat sufficient oil for deep-frying in a deep pan and when it is hot enough to brown a cube of bread in about 30 seconds, cook the falafel in batches for 4–5 minutes until crunchy and dark brown. Drain on kitchen paper, then serve with flat breads and salad.

To serve
Flat breads or pitta and salad (try Minted coleslaw on page 116, or Mr Ganoush's baba ganoush on page 34).

Serves 6

225 g/8 oz dried chickpeas, soaked overnight in water

1 small red onion, peeled and finely chopped

2 tablespoons chopped fresh parsley

2 garlic cloves, peeled and finely chopped

1 teaspoon cumin seeds

½ teaspoon ground cumin

1 teaspoon ground coriander

1 teaspoon baking powder

juice of 1 lime

sea salt and freshly ground black pepper

sunflower oil, for deep-frying

SOUPS

Mushroom and rice soup with goats' cheese

I was going to call this a congee, which is a Chinese rice soup, but it's actually a bit more like a very soft risotto. I'm using basmati rice, but it will work with any type of white rice.

1 Place the dried mushrooms in a large jug and pour over the hot stock. Set aside for 10 minutes.

2 Heat the oil in a large pan and cook the onion, garlic and thyme for 5 minutes until softened. Add the chopped fresh mushrooms and cook for a further 5 minutes. Add the rice, strain in the stock and bring to the boil.

3 Meanwhile, chop the rehydrated dried mushrooms and stir into the pan. Reduce the heat and simmer, uncovered, for 40 minutes.

4 Add salt and pepper to taste, then ladle into bowls. Cut the cheese into quarters and drop a piece into each bowl. Grind over some more black pepper and serve.

Serves 4

15 g/½ oz dried mushrooms

2 litres/3½ pints hot vegetable stock

1 tablespoon olive oil

1 small onion, peeled and finely chopped

2 garlic cloves, peeled and finely chopped

2 fresh thyme sprigs

450 g/1 lb portabella or field mushrooms, chopped

100 g/3½ oz basmati rice

100 g/3½ round firm goats' cheese

sea salt and freshly ground black pepper

Cannellini bean soup with a little bit of chorizo

Chorizo is not what you'd call a naturally healthy ingredient, but it is absolutely full of flavour and this recipe calls for only a small amount, so all in all this is very balanced, nutritious and delicious. Make sure you buy a nice chunk of chorizo sausage from the deli counter, rather than the pre-sliced packet sort.

1 Heat the oil in a large pan and cook the onion and garlic for 10 minutes until lightly browned. Add the cannellini beans and the water and bring to the boil.

2 Take off the heat and, using a hand-held blender, blitz the soup until creamy but not completely smooth. Return to the heat and simmer for 5 minutes.

3 Meanwhile, cook the diced chorizo in a non-stick frying pan for 5 minutes until it begins to crisp up and release its lovely paprika oil.

4 Stir the spinach into the soup and cook for a minute or two until wilted. Season with salt and pepper, then stir in most of the chorizo and its oils, saving a few bits to decorate the top of each bowl.

Serves 4

1 tablespoon olive oil

1 onion, peeled and chopped

4 garlic cloves, peeled and chopped

2 x 400 g/14 oz cans cannellini beans, drained

900 ml/1½ pints water

100 g/3½ oz chorizo sausage, finely diced

500 g/1 lb 2 oz young spinach leaves

sea salt and freshly ground black pepper

Bourride

A classic French fish soup is one of the most enjoyable lunches I could imagine. This one is usually served with cheesy toasts floating on the surface and sometimes a good dollop of chilli-mayonnaise. This version contains potatoes so it'll fill you up just fine without the need for toast. Or cheese. Although, of course, if you are feeling extra hungry...

1 Heat the oil in a very large pan and cook the onion and garlic for 5 minutes until softened. Add the saffron and wine, bring to the boil and bubble rapidly for 5 minutes. Dissolve the stock cube in the boiling water and add to the pan along with the potatoes and tomatoes. Bring to the boil, then reduce the heat and simmer gently for 20 minutes.

2 Add the mussels to the pan, cover with a lid and cook for 3 minutes. Add the fish and prawns to the pan and cook for 2 minutes.

3 Check that the stew is piping hot and the fish is cooked through. Discard any mussels that haven't opened. Stir in the parsley and plenty of black pepper, then ladle into large bowls and serve.

Serves 6

1 tablespoon olive oil

1 onion, peeled and roughly chopped

2 garlic cloves, quartered

a pinch of saffron

200 ml/7 fl oz dry white wine

1 chicken stock cube

750 ml/1¼ pints boiling water

2 white potatoes, peeled and cubed

4 fresh, ripe tomatoes, roughly chopped

1 kg/2¼ lb live mussels, scrubbed and bearded

500 g/1 lb 2 oz white fish, such as coley or haddock, cut into good-sized cubes

400 g/14 oz raw tiger or king prawns, unpeeled

4 tablespoons chopped fresh parsley

freshly ground black pepper

Five-minute chicken miso soup

Miso is a protein-rich paste made from fermented soy beans. It has a delicious savoury flavour and contains enzymes that are very good for digestion. Buy it in Oriental stores or from health food shops.

1 Place the noodles in a heatproof bowl and cover with a kettleful of boiling water – they are meant to be 'straight to wok', but boiling water loosens the noodles and stops them sticking to each other or breaking.

2 Pour the 1.2 litres/2 pints boiling water into a large pan and stir in the mushrooms, pak choi, chicken and miso paste. Cook gently for 3–4 minutes without boiling until the vegetables are tender.

3 Drain the noodles and divide between bowls. Ladle over the miso soup and vegetables. Scatter over the chilli and spring onions and serve.

Serves 4

150 g/5 oz pack thin 'straight-to-wok' noodles

1.2 litres/2 pints boiling water, plus a kettleful

250 g/9 oz shiitake mushrooms, sliced

6 small pak choi, halved

250 g/9 oz cooked chicken, torn into bite-sized pieces

3 tablespoons miso paste

1 red chilli, thinly sliced, seeds and all

4 spring onions, thinly sliced

Ham and parsley soup

This is a very economical but substantial and fantastic-tasting soup. Ask your butcher for the meat – it doesn't really matter if yours is a bit smaller or larger, but a lot of the flavour comes from the bone so that bit is essential, and be really generous with the parsley.

This takes a long time to simmer, but is very simple. It will freeze well in those handy 'pour and store' food bags. Serve with crusty bread.

1 Heat the butter in a large pan and cook the leeks, potatoes and rosemary for 5 minutes. Add the ham and water. Bring to the boil, then half cover the pan, reduce the heat and simmer for 1½ hours.

2 Take the pan off the heat and lift out the ham and rosemary stalks. Whiz the soup until smooth with a hand-held blender or in a liquidizer. Cut the skin and fat off the meat, then, using two forks, shred the ham from the bone (or chop it with a knife if you find it easier) and stir back into the soup – at this stage you can cool and freeze the soup.

3 Stir in the crème fraîche and season with lots of black pepper. Once piping hot, mix in the parsley and serve the soup with crusty bread.

Serves 6

a large knob of unsalted butter

2 large leeks, sliced

2 large white potatoes, about 450 g/1 lb, peeled and cubed

2 rosemary stalks

1–1.25 kg/2½ –2½ lb bone-in bacon or ham joint, such as hock or knuckle

2.5 litres/4 pints water

150 g/¼ pint carton crème fraîche

1 large bunch of fresh parsley, chopped

freshly ground black pepper

Pea and lemon soup with feta

Peas in any form are perfect for making soup. This one calls for regular green peas and I normally just use frozen – especially the sweet little petit pois. Following on from the record-breaking avocado, peas must rank very highly in terms of nutritious foods – they are among the best vegetable sources of fibre and protein and also contain vitamin C, iron and zinc.

1 Heat the oil in a large pan and cook the onion, chilli and garlic for 5 minutes until softened.

2 Add the peas, lettuce leaves and hot stock and bring to the boil, then reduce the heat and simmer for 5 minutes until the peas are tender.

3 Take off the heat and, using a hand-held blender, roughly blitz until coarsely puréed. Stir in the lemon rind and juice and season with salt and plenty of black pepper.

4 Ladle into bowls and scatter over the feta and mint leaves.

Serves 4

2 tablespoons olive oil

1 onion, peeled and roughly chopped

1 red chilli, deseeded and roughly chopped

4 garlic cloves, peeled and roughly chopped

800 g/1 lb 10 oz peas

1 small round lettuce, leaves separated and washed

1 litre/1¾ pints hot chicken or vegetable stock

grated rind and juice of 1 unwaxed lemon

75 g/3 oz feta cheese, crumbled into small pieces

a few fresh mint leaves

sea salt and freshly ground black pepper

Turkish mint soup

This is a really simple soup but the combined flavour of the mint and yoghurt is just lovely. Yoghurt can curdle if it gets too hot, so make sure you take the pan off the heat before you add it and don't reheat it. If you have leftovers, serve them chilled.

1 Heat the butter in a large pan and cook the garlic and onion for 5 minutes until softened. Stir in the courgettes and cook for a further 5 minutes.

2 Pour in the hot stock and bring to the boil, then reduce the heat and simmer for 10 minutes until the courgettes are tender. Stir in the mint and take off the heat, then, using a hand-held blender, whiz until completely smooth.

3 Stir the yoghurt into the soup and season with salt and pepper. Serve warm, or cool and serve chilled.

Serves 4

a small knob of butter

1 garlic clove, peeled and chopped

1 small onion, peeled and chopped

4 courgettes, about 750 g/ 1½ lb, sliced

750 ml/1¼ pints hot chicken or vegetable stock

1 large bunch of fresh mint leaves, roughly chopped

500 g/1 lb 2 oz Greek yoghurt

sea salt and freshly ground black pepper

Carrot and lime soup

Carrot always makes a lovely soup. It's naturally quite a sweet vegetable so I always either bring out its natural sweetness with, say, fresh orange, or, as in this case, cut against it with lime juice. Choose organic carrots and scrub rather than peel them for maximum vitamin content. Oh, and no added fat in this one!

1 Place the carrots, potato, onion, garlic and hot stock in a large pan. Bring to the boil, then reduce the heat and simmer gently for 20 minutes.

2 Take off the heat and, using a hand-held blender, whiz the soup until smooth. Season with salt and pepper, then stir in the lime juice and coriander.

3 To serve, ladle the soup into bowls and sprinkle with cumin seeds.

Serves 4

4 large carrots, grated

1 large white potato, scrubbed and grated

1 onion, peeled and finely chopped

2 garlic cloves, peeled and chopped

1.5 litres/2½ pints hot vegetable stock

juice of 2 limes

2 tablespoons chopped fresh coriander

1 teaspoon toasted cumin seeds

sea salt and freshly ground black pepper

Summer bread soup

This is essentially a fresh tomato soup and is really only worth making in the summer when the tomatoes are sweet and ripe. It is designed to be served chilled (take to work in your flask to keep it cool), but you can warm it up if you really want to.

1 Using either a heavy knife or a pestle and mortar, crush the garlic with some salt to make a smooth paste.

2 Place the tomatoes, cucumber, chilli, bread and garlic paste in a food processor and whiz until smooth. If you object to the tomato skin and seeds, pass the mixture through a sieve, otherwise tip into a large bowl.

3 Stir in the water, oil, vinegar and sugar, then add salt and pepper to taste. Chill until ready to eat.

4 To serve, chop or roughly tear the ham into pieces and ladle the soup into bowls. Scatter over the ham and a few extra drops of olive oil and enjoy.

Serves 4

2 garlic cloves, peeled

1 kg/2¼ lb ripe tomatoes

10 cm/4 inch piece of cucumber, peeled and cubed

1 red chilli, deseeded and roughly chopped

100 g/3½ oz crustless white bread

750 ml/1¼ pints water

4 tablespoons extra virgin olive oil

2 tablespoons red wine vinegar

1 teaspoon caster sugar

2 slices of Parma or Serrano ham

flaky sea salt and freshly ground black pepper

Italian lentil and pasta soup

I've been making this soup ever since I first learnt to cook. It's warm, delicious and cheap and saw me right through my college days. The combination of pasta and lentils makes a very nutritious balance indeed – protein, carbs, fibre, vitamins and plenty of flavour in every bowlful. The bacon is nice but not essential.

1 Heat the oil in a large pan and cook the onion, garlic, celery, carrot and bacon for 5–8 minutes until the onion has softened. Stir in the rosemary, lentils and tomato and cook for a couple of minutes more.

2 Stir in the hot water and simmer, uncovered, for 20–30 minutes until the lentils are tender and the liquid is quite reduced. Cook them for longer if you have time – it's best when the lentils start to break down a little.

3 Cook the pasta in a separate pan of boiling water according to the packet instructions. Drain and stir into the cooked lentils. Check the seasoning and serve. (This isn't as good when left to cool and reheated the next day as the pasta tends to absorb the liquid if left for a few hours, so make sure you eat it all at once.)

Serves 4

2 tablespoons olive oil

1 onion, peeled and finely chopped

2 garlic cloves, peeled and finely chopped

1 celery stalk, finely chopped

1 carrot, peeled and finely chopped

1–2 rashers streaky bacon, chopped

1 fresh rosemary or thyme stalk

200 g/7 oz dried green or brown lentils

1 ripe tomato, roughly chopped

1 litre/1¾ pints hot water

75 g/3 oz small pasta shapes (tubetti are my favourite for this)

sea salt and freshly ground black pepper

Moroccan-spiced red onion soup

I subscribe to a weekly organic vegetable box scheme and always seem to have tons of onions left over at the end of the month, but this is the perfect way to use them up – you can use regular brown onions, too, if you've got them. I guess it's a spin on the classic French onion soup and as such is quite light.

1 Heat the oil in a large pan and gently cook the onions for 15 minutes until golden and softened.

2 Add the cumin and cinnamon and cook for a further 5 minutes, then add the hot stock and simmer for 10 minutes.

3 Meanwhile, brush the bread with the oil and sprinkle with the paprika. Pop under a low grill for 8 minutes or so until golden and crispy – if using pitta, split them in half first.

4 Stir the orange rind and juice and the parsley into the soup, then ladle into bowls. Break the crispy bread into pieces and scatter over the soup. Serve swiftly.

Serves 4

2 tablespoons vegetable oil

6 red onions, peeled and sliced

1 teaspoon cumin seeds

2 cinnamon sticks

1.5 litres/2½ pints hot chicken stock

grated rind and juice of 1 large unwaxed orange

2 tablespoons chopped fresh parsley

To serve

1 large flat bread or 2 pittas

1 teaspoon vegetable oil

1 teaspoon smoked paprika

Chilli cornmeal soup

This is a sort of Mexican hotchpotch using all the obvious ingredients, but made interesting with the added cornmeal to give it some body. It'll make you feel happy and sunny on a cold, wet evening. If you're feeling really fed up, leave out the lime and stir a handful of grated cheese into each bowlful – comfort food at its best.

1 Heat the oil in a pan and cook the onion, garlic and half the chopped chillies for 5 minutes until softened. Add the chilli powder and cook for 1 minute more.

2 Stir in the cornmeal or polenta, the tomatoes, beans and stock. Bring to the boil, stirring from time to time, then reduce the heat and simmer gently for 20 minutes.

3 Season the soup and add the lime rind and juice to taste. Ladle into bowls and top each with some of the remaining green chillies and the coriander leaves.

Serves 4

1 tablespoon olive oil

1 onion, peeled and chopped

2 garlic cloves, peeled and chopped

4 green chillies, deseeded and chopped

1–2 teaspoons hot chilli powder

50 g/2 oz cornmeal or polenta

400 g/14 oz can chopped plum tomatoes

400 g/14 oz can kidney beans, drained

1.5 litres/2½ pints hot vegetable stock

grated rind and juice of 1 unwaxed lime

a handful of fresh coriander leaves

sea salt and freshly ground black pepper

Chickpea purée with crispy shallots

I love chickpeas and they love us, too. They're an excellent source of protein, fibre and vitamins and taste lovely, especially in this soft smooth soup.

1 Heat the olive oil in a large pan and cook the onion and garlic for 5 minutes until they start to turn translucent. Add the cumin seeds and harissa paste and cook for another minute, then add the chickpeas, potato and water. Bring to the boil, then reduce the heat and simmer gently for 30 minutes.

2 For the crispy onions, separate the shallot slices onto a double layer of kitchen paper and sprinkle with salt. Heat 1 cm/½ inch of vegetable oil in a large frying pan until hot, then pat the onions dry with the paper and cook for a few minutes until brown and crispy. Drain with a slotted spoon and place on kitchen paper to absorb any excess oil.

3 Using a hand-held blender, whiz the soup until smooth. At this point you can set the soup aside for serving later if you want to. When ready to eat, warm the soup through, but do not boil again. Stir through the yoghurt and coriander, add salt and pepper to taste and serve, or whiz again to blend in the herb.

4 Ladle into bowls, sprinkle over the crispy shallots and serve.

Serves 4

1 tablespoon olive oil

1 onion, peeled and roughly chopped

3 garlic cloves, peeled and roughly chopped

1 teaspoon cumin seeds

2–3 teaspoons harissa paste or other chilli sauce

2 x 400 g/14 oz cans chickpeas, drained

1 white potato, peeled and diced

1.5 litres/2½ pints water

150 g carton Greek yoghurt

1 bunch of fresh coriander, chopped

sea salt and freshly ground black pepper

For the crispy shallots

4 shallots, peeled and thinly sliced

sea salt

vegetable oil, for shallow-frying

Simple roasted tomato soup

Roasted tomato soup is a modern classic. It is by far the best way to make a tomato soup as the roasting process really intensifies and sweetens the flavour.

1 Preheat the oven to 180°C/350°F/mark 4. Place the tomatoes and garlic in a roasting tin. Scatter over the basil and drizzle over the olive oil. Season and roast for 40–50 minutes until the tomatoes are softened and a little charred. Take the garlic out of the pan if it starts to get too dark – much past dark golden – as it can taste a little bitter.

2 Meanwhile, place the stock and potatoes in a large pan. Bring to the boil, cover, and simmer for 15–20 minutes until tender.

3 Slip the garlic out of its papery skin and add to the pan, along with the tomatoes and basil. Using a hand-held blender, whiz until thick and fairly smooth.

4 Season to taste then ladle into bowls and serve scattered with Pecorino croutons.

Serves 4

1 kg/2¼ lb ripe tomatoes, halved

1 head of garlic, halved horizontally

a handful of fresh basil leaves

2 tablespoons olive oil

1.5 litres/2½ pints hot vegetable stock

1 white potato, peeled and diced

sea salt and freshly ground black pepper

Pecorino croutons (page 30), to serve

Simple Thai chicken soup

You don't need to buy one of those cartons of chilled soup when you can make this fresh version at home in about 20 minutes. It uses only supermarket ingredients and is bursting with flavour!

1 Place the noodles in a heatproof bowl and pour over a kettleful of boiling water.

2 Put half the chillies, the ginger and hot stock in a large pan. Lightly flatten the lemongrass stalk and add to the pan. Bring to the boil, then reduce the heat and simmer gently for 5–10 minutes.

3 Add the chicken, coconut cream and mushrooms and simmer for 3 minutes. Add the pak choi and simmer for a further 2 minutes.

4 Drain the noodles and divide between bowls. Top each pile of noodles with a handful of beansprouts.

5 Season the soup with the lime juice and fish sauce, if using, then ladle into the bowls. Scatter over the spring onions and the remaining chillies and serve hot.

Serves 4

100 g/4 oz flat rice noodles

3 hot red chillies, deseeded and finely chopped

1 large knob of fresh root ginger, peeled and shredded

1.5 litres/2½ pints hot chicken stock

1 lemongrass stalk

2 large skinless, boneless chicken breasts, cut into strips

200 g/7 oz coconut cream

200 g/7 oz shiitake or button mushrooms, thinly sliced

4 pak choi, halved

75 g/3 oz beansprouts

juice of 1 lime

a splash of fish sauce (if you have any)

2 spring onions, shredded

Sweet potato Cullen Skink

It's that famous haddock and potato soup named after the Scottish fishing village called Cullen. As far as I'm aware, skink traditionally means meat soup – except, of course, in this case. Traditionally, Finnan haddie – smoked haddock from the fishing village of Findon, near Aberdeen – is used, but good-quality, undyed smoked haddock will do just fine. My untraditional version uses sweet potato, which matches the salty fish flavour very well indeed.

For a real treat, poach an egg and drop one into each bowl before serving.

1 Melt the butter in a large pan and cook the onion for 5 minutes until softened. Add the fish – you may need to cut it so it fits into the pan. Pour over the milk and bring to the boil, then reduce the heat, cover the pan and simmer gently for 10 minutes.

2 Meanwhile, peel, cube and cook the sweet potatoes in a pan of boiling water for 10–15 minutes until tender. Drain and mash roughly.

3 Once the fish is cooked, lift it out of the pan and break into large flakes. Stir the mashed sweet potato into the pan along with the flaked fish and the parsley. Gently heat through, check the seasoning, then ladle into bowls (pop a poached egg into each first, if using) and serve.

Poaching eggs

Crack the eggs into a pan of just-simmering water and cook for 2 minutes. Take off the heat and leave to sit for 5 minutes until the whites are set, but the yolks are still a little soft.

Serves 4

a small knob of butter

1 small onion, peeled and finely chopped

800 g/1 lb 10 oz undyed smoked haddock fillets, skinned and boned

1.2 litres/2 pints whole milk

2 sweet potatoes

2 tablespoons chopped fresh parsley

sea salt and freshly ground black pepper

4 poached eggs, to serve (optional)

Mega Fillers

Parsley Frittata

I've kept this very simple because I love the flavour of parsley. You can, however, dress it up by adding, for example, torn ham or diced cheese. It's great slipped out of the pan and eaten hot with a quick tomato salad, or cooled, wrapped in foil and packed up for lunch (or breakfast) the next day.

1 Place the bread in a bowl, cover with cold water and leave for a few minutes.

2 Meanwhile, pop the garlic, chilli and parsley (leaves only) into a food processor and whiz until finely chopped. Drain the bread, lightly squeeze out any excess water, but leaving it quite soggy, add to the food processor and whiz again until well blended.

3 Crack the eggs into a large bowl and beat well together. Add the parsley and bread mixture, the Parmesan and spring onions, then season with salt and plenty of black pepper.

4 Heat the oil in a 20 cm/8 inch non-stick skillet. Pour the eggs into the hot pan and cook for 1 minute or so, stirring until the egg begins to set, then cook on the lowest heat for 6–7 minutes until the egg is almost completely set. Preheat the grill to medium.

5 Place the pan under the preheated grill for 2–3 minutes until the frittata is golden brown and cooked through. Slide onto a chopping board and cut into wedges. Serve with a tomato salad, Parma ham and rocket.

Serves 4

1 thick slice of a day or two-day old rough white bread, about 50 g/2 oz

2 garlic cloves, peeled and roughly chopped

1 red chilli, deseeded and roughly chopped

1 large bunch of fresh parsley, preferably curly but flat-leaf is fine

6 eggs

2 tablespoons freshly grated Parmesan cheese

4 spring onions, thinly sliced

1 tablespoon olive oil

sea salt and freshly ground black pepper

tomato salad, and maybe some sliced Parma ham and rocket, to serve

Myriam's milky macaroni with poached apples

My Swiss friend Myriam presents the cookery programme on Swiss National Radio. She describes this as 'the perfect dish for a rainy day', and says the poached apples help to digest 'the fancy cheese and will save you the dessert'. The apples are still delicious the day after. Myriam says 'this dish is for four people; or one with a broken heart...'

1 For the poached apples, cut the apples in half and remove the core, then cut into quarters. Put the apples in a small pan, add a squeeze of lemon juice and cover with water. Bring to the boil, then reduce the heat and simmer for about 5 minutes until they are soft. Add some more lemon juice and the vanilla sugar to taste, and leave to cool for a while.

2 Cook the macaroni in a pan of boiling water. In the meantime, melt the butter in a frying pan, then add the onion and fry until soft and golden brown. Take off the heat, but keep the onions warm.

3 Heat the milk in a small pan and spice it with the bouillon powder, some freshly grated nutmeg and black pepper.

4 Drain the hot macaroni and put half of it in a large serving dish. Evenly sprinkle half the grated cheese over it, then cover with the remaining macaroni and top with the rest of the cheese. Pour the milk mixture over and add more nutmeg, if desired. Spread the fried onions over it, cover with a lid or some foil and then let it rest for just 4–5 minutes to enable the cheese to melt.

To serve, place the macaroni on the table and pass the poached apples.

Serves 4

400 g/14 oz macaroni

1 teaspoon butter

1 large white onion, peeled

200 ml/7 fl oz whole milk

a large pinch of vegetable bouillon powder

freshly grated nutmeg

200 g/7 oz Gruyère cheese, grated

freshly ground black pepper

For the poached apples

2 apples

juice of ½ lemon

½ teaspoon vanilla sugar (optional)

Thai spiced pork and rice noodles

This is an absolute classic, but one I'll never grow bored of. Traditionally the pork is served piled onto or rolled into lettuce leaves, but I've chosen instead to toss my leaves in with the mixture.

1 Place the noodles in a large heatproof bowl and pour over a kettleful of boiling water.

2 Heat the oil in a wok until smoking, then stir-fry the pork and garlic for 5 minutes until golden and cooked through. Tip into a large serving bowl.

3 Mix the fish sauce with the lime juice and chilli sauce and stir into the hot pork with the onion, beansprouts and chopped chillies. Drain the noodles, stir into the bowl and leave to settle for 5–10 minutes.

4 Stir in the lettuce and herbs and serve warm.

Serves 4

100 g/3½ oz vermicelli rice noodles

1 tablespoon groundnut or sunflower oil

750 g/1½ lb lean minced pork

2 garlic cloves, peeled and crushed

2 tablespoons fish sauce

juice of 2 limes

2 tablespoons sweet chilli sauce

1 red onion, peeled and thinly sliced

100 g/3½ oz beansprouts

2 hot red chillies, finely chopped, seeds and all

2 little gem lettuce, leaves separated and torn

a large handful of fresh mint leaves

a large handful of fresh basil leaves

Prawn udon noodles

I love udon noodles. They're made from wheat and are usually very thick and quite rounded strands – good for slurping! They can be bought dried from specialist stores, but are available in most supermarkets cooked and vacuum-packed in 'straight-to-wok' packs. Make sure you use the Oriental chilli oil with shrimp paste in it.

1 Place the noodles in a large heatproof bowl and cover with a kettleful of boiling water – they are meant to be 'straight to wok', but boiling water loosens the noodles and stops them sticking to each other or breaking. Leave for 5 minutes, then drain well.

2 Heat the oil in a large wok. Once it starts to smoke, add the noodles and prawns and stir-fry over the highest heat for 4–5 minutes until the prawns are pink and curled.

3 Keeping the heat at highest, stir in the chillies, spring onions, beansprouts, soy sauce, vinegar and chilli oil. Cook for a couple of minutes until piping hot, then turn out onto plates. Scatter over the peanuts and coriander leaves and eat.

Serves 4

2 x 150 g/5 oz packs 'straight-to-wok' udon noodles

1 tablespoon sunflower oil

500 g/1 lb 2 oz raw shelled tiger prawns, deveined

2 red chillies, thinly sliced, seeds and all

4 spring onions, sliced

100 g/3½ oz beansprouts

1 tablespoon soy sauce

1 teaspoon rice or wine vinegar

1 teaspoon chilli oil

50 g pack salted peanuts, finely chopped

a handful of fresh coriander leaves

Holiday squid and potatoes

I love squid! It reminds me, firstly, of my mum's kitchen where she always dusts the rings in flour, dips them in egg and fries them in olive oil, and, secondly, of being on holiday. We don't get served squid often enough in northern Europe, but in Italy, Portugal and Spain every pavement restaurant and café has it on the menu. Serve with plain boiled potatoes and use the back of your fork to mash them into the lovely juices. The perfect lunch and good for you, too.

1 Place the garlic, tomatoes, basil and oil in a small pan and cook for 10 minutes until the tomatoes are pulpy. Pour in the wine and bubble rapidly for 5 minutes, then stir in a splash of water.

2 Add the squid and cook for just a couple of minutes until it turns white and loses its translucency. Stir in the capers and parsley and add the lemon juice and seasoning to taste. Serve straightaway with boiled potatoes (or crusty bread).

Best boiled potatoes

Choose small white-skinned potatoes and put them whole into a pan of cold water. Bring to the boil, then reduce the heat and simmer until tender. Drain and, when just cool enough to handle, peel off the skins. Toss with a tiny splash of olive oil and a little sea salt.

Serves 2

4 garlic cloves, peeled and finely chopped

4 ripe tomatoes, finely chopped

a handful of fresh basil leaves

2 tablespoons olive oil

100 ml/3½ fl oz red wine

400 g/14 oz cleaned squid, cut into rings

1 tablespoon capers, rinsed

4 tablespoons roughly chopped fresh parsley

juice of ½ lemon

sea salt and freshly ground black pepper

boiled whole potatoes, to serve

Saffron-baked rice and chicken

This is sort of a cross between a risotto and a biriyani. It's a one-pot dish (which are always my favourites – life's too short for more than 5 minutes at the sink) and uses warm Med flavours and basmati rice with its elegant, separate grains. Pop it in the oven and forget all about it for about half an hour.

1 Preheat the oven to 200°C/400°F/mark 6. Stir the saffron into the hot stock and set aside.

2 Heat the oil in a large casserole or roasting tin and cook the chicken, onion and garlic for 5 minutes or so until the onion has softened a little. Add the paprika and rosemary and cook for a couple of minutes more.

3 Stir in the tomatoes, rice, vinegar and warm stock. Cover and pop in the oven for 20–30 minutes until the rice is tender and all the stock has been absorbed. Stir through the parsley and dish up.

Serves 4

a large pinch of saffron

750 ml/1¼ pints hot chicken stock

1 tablespoon olive oil

8 cubed skinless boneless chicken thighs or 4 cubed skinless boneless breasts

1 red onion, peeled and thinly sliced

2 garlic cloves, peeled and thinly sliced

2 teaspoons smoked paprika

1 rosemary stalk, broken into sprigs

4 tomatoes, roughly chopped

400 g/14 oz basmati rice

1 teaspoon balsamic vinegar

1 bunch of fresh flat-leaf parsley, roughly chopped

Pot-roast chicken with lemon and potatoes

Most of the recipes in this book are quick to cook; this one takes a little longer, but doesn't ask for much time in terms of preparation. Just pop it in the oven and come back to it later. Ask the butcher to chop up the bird for you if you're not sure about doing it yourself. The crème fraîche is not essential, but is very nice.

1 Preheat the oven to 200°C/400°F/mark 6. Place the chicken pieces, lemon, onion, garlic, potatoes and tarragon in a large ovenproof dish. Add some salt and pepper, then pour over the hot stock – it should come about halfway up the dish and some of the chicken and potatoes should be sitting out of the liquid.

2 Roast in the oven for 45 minutes until the chicken is cooked through and golden on the surface. Lift out and discard the lemon. Stir in the crème fraîche and serve.

Serves 4

1 large chicken, cut into 8 pieces

1 small thin-skinned unwaxed lemon, pierced once or twice with a knife

1 onion, peeled and finely chopped

4 garlic cloves, peeled and halved

4 red-skinned potatoes, peeled and cubed

a small handful of fresh tarragon leaves

500 ml/17 fl oz hot chicken stock

2 tablespoons crème fraîche

sea salt and freshly ground black pepper

Pork and charmoula burgers

Charmoula is a Moroccan spiced sauce or marinade and it does a brilliant job of livening up pork, which can be a bit on the bland side.

1 Using either a heavy knife or a pestle and mortar, crush the garlic with some salt to make a smooth paste. Stir in the paprika, cayenne, cumin and vinegar to make the charmoula.

2 Mix the pork with the charmoula and coriander and shape into 8 patties. Cook in a non-stick frying pan for 5–6 minutes on each side until nicely browned and cooked through. Serve hot with the lemon wedges, some salad and chutney or nice rice (see below).

Nice rice

There's a wonderful Lebanese takeaway on my local high street where the hot skewers of spiced lamb always come with lots of nice extras such as pickled green chillies, crispy white cabbage salad, yoghurty dips and, best of all, their reddish short-grained rice. I'm not sure how they make it, but it is a delicious accompaniment to all grilled meats. For my version, I cook basmati rice in boiling water with a finely chopped tomato, a tiny pinch of saffron and a small knob of butter.

Serves 4

2 garlic cloves, peeled

1 teaspoon paprika

1 teaspoon cayenne

1 teaspoon ground cumin

1 tablespoon red wine vinegar

500 g/1 lb 2 oz lean minced pork

2 tablespoons roughly chopped fresh coriander leaves

flaky sea salt

lemon wedges, for squeezing over

Spinach and goats' cheese tart

Not much can beat a real homemade tart and this one takes no short cuts, although if you wish, do use ready-made shortcrust pastry. This is ideal for making the day before, but store in a cool, dry place rather than the fridge if you want to avoid a soggy bottom.

1 Preheat the oven to 200°C/400°F/mark 6. Place both flours, the butter and ½ teaspoon salt in a food processor and whiz until the mixture forms fine crumbs. Pour in the cold water and pulse again to form a firm dough.

2 Roll the pastry out on a floured surface and use to line a 23 cm/9 inch loose-bottomed tart tin. Prick the base, fill with crumpled foil and bake in the oven for 10 minutes, then remove the foil. Lower the oven to 180°C/350°F/mark 4 and return the case to the oven for 3–4 minutes.

3 Wash the spinach well and cook in a pan or microwave until wilted, then squeeze out any excess water. Heat the butter in a frying pan and cook the garlic for 2 minutes until softened but not coloured. Stir in the spinach to coat it in the garlic butter, then remove from the heat.

4 Beat together the cream, milk, whole eggs and egg yolks and chilli flakes until well blended. Add a little salt and pepper.

5 Arrange the spinach and cheese in the tart case and pour over the egg mixture. Bake in the oven for 25 minutes until golden and just set. Carefully remove the tart from the tin, cut into slices and serve while still warm.

Serves 6

100 g/3½ oz plain flour, plus extra for dusting

100 g/3½ oz wholemeal flour

100 g/3½ oz chilled butter, diced

3 tablespoons very cold water

For the filling

250 g/9 oz fresh spinach

a small knob of butter

1 garlic clove, peeled and thinly sliced

142 ml/4½ fl oz carton soured cream

300 ml/½ pint whole milk

2 large eggs plus 2 yolks

½ teaspoon dried chilli flakes

200 g/7 oz firm rinded goats' cheese, diced

sea salt and freshly ground black pepper

Barley and butternut risotto

This takes a while to cook as the vegetables are roasted separately, but the flavour they develop is worth the extra effort. This is fantastic packed into lunch boxes and eaten as a cold salad the next day.

1 Preheat the oven to 200°C/400°F/mark 6. Toss the carrot and butternut squash with 2 tablespoons of the oil and some salt on a baking sheet and spread out in an even layer. Roast in the oven until golden and tender, about 25 minutes.

2 Meanwhile, heat the remaining oil in a large pan. Cook the onion and garlic for a couple of minutes, then add the barley and cook, stirring occasionally, until the vegetables soften a bit, about 5 minutes.

3 Pour in the wine and cook, stirring frequently, until the liquid is absorbed. Add the hot stock and thyme, reduce the heat and simmer fairly gently for 30–35 minutes until the liquid is absorbed and the barley is tender but still slightly firm.

4 Stir in the roasted vegetables and divide between bowls. Scatter over the Parmesan and serve.

Serves 4

1 medium carrot, peeled and sliced

1 small butternut squash, peeled, deseeded and cut into 1.5 cm/¾ inch chunks

4 tablespoons extra virgin olive oil

1 onion, peeled and chopped

2 garlic cloves, peeled and roughly chopped

200 g/7 oz pearl barley

200 ml/7 fl oz dry white wine

750 ml/1¼ pints hot chicken or vegetable stock

2 fresh thyme sprigs

sea salt

freshly grated Parmesan cheese, to serve

Curried kipper fish cakes

I see no reason to be snooty about boil-in-the-bag kippers. I always keep a bag in the freezer for emergencies and love the fact I can boil the kippers and my eggs in the same pan if I want a quick kedgeree for Sunday breakfast. Of course, if you have a good local fishmonger with gorgeous fresh kippers, you must use them. A chopped hard-boiled egg makes a lovely addition.

1 Cook the potatoes in a large pan of boiling water until tender. Drain and mash thoroughly.

2 Meanwhile, cook the kippers according to the packet instructions, or place in a bowl, cover with a kettleful of boiling water and set aside for 10 minutes.

3 Stir the chives or spring onions, the curry paste and peas into the potatoes. Skin the kippers and break the flakes into the potato mixture, then gently fold together. With floured hands, shape the mixture into 6–8 cakes.

4 Brush a large non-stick frying pan with oil and cook the fish cakes for 5 minutes on each side until crisp, golden and piping hot. Serve with salad leaves.

Serves 4–6

750 g/1½ lb floury white potatoes, peeled

400 g/14 oz kipper fillets

1 bunch of fresh chives or 4 spring onions, finely chopped

1 tablespoon curry paste

50 g/2 oz frozen peas, thawed

plain flour, for dusting

1 tablespoon sunflower oil

salad leaves, to serve

Fiery basil and broccoli penne

This recipe uses my favourite 'double basil' method. The basil goes in at the beginning with the bacon where the flavour cooks in wonderfully and then it's added again at the end for a fresh, vibrant flavour. Yum. Try, too, with cauliflower instead of the broccoli.

1 Cook the pasta in a large pan of boiling salted water for 5 minutes. Add the broccoli and continue to cook until the pasta is just cooked and the broccoli is just a little bit overcooked.

2 Heat the oil in a small frying pan and cook the onion, bacon, chillies, garlic and half the basil for 8 minutes or so until the onions are nicely golden and the pasta is ready.

3 Drain the pasta and broccoli (use a large sieve as you will lose a lot of the broccoli through the big holes of a colander) and return to the pan. Stir in the bacon and onion mixture, the remaining fresh basil leaves and plenty of freshly ground black pepper. Squeeze in the lemon juice and serve with the grated cheese.

Serves 4

500 g/1 lb 2 oz pack penne or fusilli

1 small head of broccoli, cut into small florets

1–2 tablespoons olive oil

1 small onion, chopped

2 rashers streaky bacon, chopped

2 hot red chillies, thinly sliced

2 garlic cloves, peeled and thinly sliced

a large bunch of fresh basil leaves

juice of ½ lemon

sea salt and freshly ground black pepper

freshly grated Parmesan or pecorino cheese, to serve

Stir-fried mushrooms with ginger and greens

I'm quite fussy about how I take my mushrooms – those white buttons, in particular, taste of nothing at all and don't have a very nice texture either. Some good chestnut mushrooms, however, cooked with ginger, chillies and soy sauce are a different deal altogether. For your greens choose an Oriental leaf such as pak choi or choi sum, young leaf spinach or baby chard.

Serve with plain rice or noodles and, if you like them, scatter over some toasted cashews.

1 Put your wok on to get very hot. Meanwhile, mix all the ingredients for the dressing in a bowl and put to one side.

2 Once the wok is very hot, add the groundnut or sunflower oil, then stir-fry the ginger, garlic and chilli for 20 seconds. Add the mushrooms, spring onions and greens and stir-fry for a few minutes, until the mushrooms have taken on some colour and the greens have wilted.

3 Pour in the dressing, take off the heat and stir in the basil or coriander. Eat straightaway.

Serves 2

1 tablespoon groundnut or sunflower oil

3.5 cm/1½ inch piece of fresh root ginger, peeled and shredded

1 garlic clove, peeled and thinly sliced

1 hot red chilli, thinly sliced

250 g/9 oz largish chestnut mushrooms, halved

6 spring onions, thickly sliced

a bowl of green leaves (see above)

a few fresh Thai parsley or basil or coriander leaves

For the dressing

2 tablespoons light soy sauce

a pinch of caster sugar

a pinch of flaky sea salt

1 teaspoon rice or wine vinegar

1 teaspoon sesame oil

1 tablespoon cold water

Asparagus and lemon rice

Brown rice is far more satisfying than its polished white counterparts. It's chewy and nutty and also takes longer to digest so you get a good, slow release of energy. I've served it here with classic risotto flavourings and the result is delicious.

1 Heat the oil in a pan and cook the onion and garlic for 5 minutes until softened. Stir in the rice and cook for a minute or two, then pour over the boiling water and simmer for 30 minutes until the grains are tender.

2 Add the asparagus, cover and continue to cook for a further 5–7 minutes until the rice and asparagus are tender and all the liquid has been absorbed.

3 Stir in the lemon rind and juice and the mascarpone and season to taste.

Serves 4

1 tablespoon olive oil

1 small onion, peeled and finely chopped

2 garlic cloves, peeled and finely chopped

300 g/11 oz brown rice

1 litre/1¾ pints boiling water

300 g/11 oz thick asparagus spears, halved

grated rind and juice of 1 unwaxed lemon

2–3 tablespoons mascarpone or other soft cheese

sea salt and freshly ground black pepper

Big Salads

Chickpea salad with flat bread

This is very simple, but the combination of flavours makes it really enjoyable to eat. It's even better, though slightly stronger tasting, the next day. I've dressed this with avocado oil of which I am a fan (vitamin E and lovely flavour), but use olive oil if you'd rather.

1 Tip the chickpeas into a large bowl and stir in the feta, onion and coriander leaves. In a small bowl, whisk together the cumin seeds, chilli flakes, oil and lime rind and juice. Season with salt and pepper, then pour over the chickpeas, mixing well together. Leave to settle for 10 minutes if you've got the time.

2 Toast the flat breads or tortillas until crisp and dark golden. Spoon on the salad and eat.

Serves 2

400 g/14 oz can chickpeas, drained and rinsed

100 g/3½ oz feta cheese, crumbled

1 small red onion, peeled and finely chopped

a handful of fresh coriander leaves

1 teaspoon toasted cumin seeds

a large pinch of crushed chilli flakes

2 tablespoons avocado oil

juice and grated rind of 1 unwaxed lime

2 Lebanese flat breads or flour tortillas

sea salt and freshly ground black pepper

Egg and potato salad

Boiled eggs and potatoes are always going to make a lovely salad. This one also has capers, olives and anchovies and is dressed with a gorgeous mustard vinaigrette.

1 Put two pans of water on to boil – one small and one large. Cook the potatoes in the large pan for 20 minutes until tender. Add the eggs to the other pan and cook for 8 minutes, then cool, shell and quarter them.

2 Next, make the vinaigrette. Place the garlic and ½ teaspoon sea salt in a mini food processor and whiz to a paste. Whiz in the mustard and vinegars and then the oil until well blended. Check the seasoning, adding salt and pepper to taste.

3 Drain the potatoes and place in a large bowl. Stir in the vinaigrette and shallots and leave to cool for 10 minutes.

4 Mix in the olives, anchovies, capers and parsley and divide between serving bowls or plates. Top with the eggs and serve while still warm.

Serves 4

1 kg/2¼ lb Anya or other new potatoes, halved if large

4 large eggs

4 shallots, peeled and finely chopped

75 g/3 oz stuffed green olives, sliced

50 g/2 oz can anchovies in olive oil, drained and roughly chopped

4 tablespoons small capers, rinsed

1 large bunch of fresh parsley, roughly chopped

For the vinaigrette

2 garlic cloves, peeled

1 teaspoon English mustard powder

1 tablespoon balsamic vinegar

1 tablespoon sherry or wine vinegar

100 ml/3½ fl oz extra virgin olive oil

sea salt and freshly ground black pepper

Soba, watermelon and feta salad

Soba noodles are made with buckwheat and are traditionally served either hot in soups or cold in salads. They can be replaced in this gorgeous salad with rice noodles, if preferred.

1 Cook the noodles in a pan of lightly salted boiling water for 3–4 minutes until tender. Tip them into a colander and place under cold running water until they are completely cold. Then give the colander a good shake to get rid of any excess water.

2 Gently toss the cooled noodles with the watermelon, coriander leaves, feta, spring onions and sesame seeds. Whisk together the lime juice, oils and black pepper and drizzle over the salad. Serve chilled.

Serves 4

150 g/5 oz soba noodles

¼ watermelon, cut into cubes

1 bunch of fresh coriander leaves

200 g/7 oz block feta cheese, roughly diced

2 spring onions, finely chopped

1 tablespoon toasted sesame seeds

juice of 1 plump lime

1 tablespoon olive oil

1 teaspoon sesame oil

sea salt and freshly ground black pepper

Vinegar-rubbed lamb salad with herb couscous

Rubbing vinegar into the lamb produces a lovely flavour and has a tenderizing effect. Lamb fillet is an expensive cut, but it's also very lean, which is essential for a just-warm salad.

1 Place the lamb in a dish with 2 tablespoons of the vinegar, the sugar, a little salt and the garlic. Using your hands, massage the flavours into the lamb, then set aside for 5–10 minutes.

2 Meanwhile, pour the hot stock over the couscous and set aside. Preheat the grill to medium.

3 Discard the garlic and cook the lamb under the grill, turning from time to time for 12–20 minutes. Leave the lamb to rest for 5 minutes, then slice.

4 Fluff up the couscous with a fork, then stir in the lamb's resting juices, the remaining vinegar, the oil, herbs, tomato and shallot. (I like to leave this all to cool down a little and serve just warm, but it can be served hotter.)

5 Stir the rocket and lamb into the couscous and serve with the yoghurt or tzatziki.

Serves 2

300 g/11 oz lamb fillet

3 tablespoons red wine vinegar

a pinch of sugar

2 garlic cloves, peeled and quartered

175 ml/6 fl oz hot chicken stock

150 g/5 oz couscous

2 tablespoons olive oil

2 tablespoons chopped fresh mint leaves

2 tablespoons chopped fresh parsley

1 ripe tomato, finely chopped

1 shallot, peeled and finely chopped

50 g/2 oz wild rocket

sea salt

Greek yoghurt or tzatziki, to serve

Rosemary-roasted chicken and sweet potato salad

This is simple to make and fantastic served warm, or chilled and packed into a box for a perfect picnic or desktop lunch. If you feel like pushing this recipe a bit further, top with a few cubes of gentle blue cheese such as Dolcelatte or a mild Gorgonzola.

1 Preheat the oven to 220°C/425°F/mark 7. Place the chicken pieces skin-side up in a large shallow roasting tin with the sweet potatoes and tomatoes. Tuck in the garlic and rosemary. Drizzle over 1 tablespoon of the oil, then sprinkle with salt and pepper and the fennel seeds if you have them. Roast in the oven for 20–25 minutes until the chicken is golden and cooked through and the sweet potatoes are tender.

2 Dress with the lime juice and remaining oil, then leave to cool in the tin for a good 10 minutes.

3 If eating warm, toss with the watercress and divide between bowls. If serving cold, dress the chicken with the oil and lime juice as before, but leave to cool completely before tossing with the watercress.

Serves 4

4 skin-on boneless chicken thighs, each cut into 6

2 large sweet potatoes, peeled and cut into chunks

100 g/3½ oz cherry tomatoes

4 whole unpeeled garlic cloves

4 rosemary stalks, broken into sprigs

2 tablespoons olive oil

1 teaspoon fennel seeds (not essential but nice if you have them)

juice of 1 lime

1 bunch of watercress

sea salt and freshly ground black pepper

Anchovy panzanella

Panzanella is a classic Tuscan salad traditionally made with day-old bread. This version is made special by the addition of fresh oil-and-herb-marinated anchovy fillets – you can buy these in some supermarkets and from the counter in most delis.

1 Preheat the oven to 200°C/400°F/mark 6. Scatter the bread cubes in a single layer onto a large non-stick baking sheet. Bake in the oven for 12 minutes until crunchy and golden.

2 Arrange the tomatoes on a second tray and bake for 10 minutes until the skins split and the tomatoes begin to soften. Using a pair of scissors, snip the vines between each tomato to separate them.

3 To make the dressing, drain the oily marinade from the anchovies or seafood salad into a bowl. Add the tomato paste and vinegar, then use a fork to lightly whisk them together.

4 Arrange the bread, tomatoes, chilli peppers, anchovy fillets or seafood salad and the basil on a large serving platter. Drizzle over the dressing and serve.

Serves 4

1 large ciabatta loaf, cubed

450 g/1 lb cherry tomatoes on the vine

200 g/7 oz pack marinated fresh anchovy fillets or seafood salad in oil

1 tablespoon sun-dried tomato paste

1 tablespoon red wine vinegar

375 g/13 oz jar sweet pickled chilli peppers, drained

1 bunch of fresh basil

Hot-smoked salmon with minted coleslaw

Hot-smoked salmon is now readily available and is great for salads and sandwiches. The soft oily salmon is really well complemented by the crisp and crunchy white cabbage.

1 Using either a heavy knife or a pestle and mortar, crush the garlic with some salt to make a smooth paste. Stir in the lime juice, oil and caraway seeds to make a dressing.

2 Place the cabbage, onion and mint in a large bowl and toss with the dressing. Divide between plates and top with the salmon, either whole or flaked.

Serves 4

1 small garlic clove, peeled

juice of 1 lime

3 tablespoons extra virgin olive oil

1 teaspoon caraway seeds

1 small white cabbage, about 250 g/9 oz, shredded

1 small red onion, peeled and thinly sliced

1 bunch of fresh mint leaves, roughly torn

4 x 125–150 g/4–5 oz fillets hot-smoked salmon

flaky sea salt

Green lentil salad with rocket and crispy bacon

Green lentils make a lovely salad base and go particularly well with the crispy, salty bacon and peppery rocket. This recipe uses canned lentils for speed, but to cook your own, use 125 g (4 oz) dried green lentils and boil for 20 minutes until tender.

1 Place the bacon on a grill rack and cook under a medium grill for about 8 minutes, turning once, until crisp.

2 Meanwhile, heat the oil in a frying pan and cook the onion, garlic and rosemary for 5 minutes. Add the lentils and heat until just warmed through. Stir in the crème fraîche, mixing until it melts to coat the lentils, then stir in the vinegar and take off the heat. Check the seasoning, adding salt and pepper to taste.

3 Toss in the leaves and divide between two bowls. Break the bacon into pieces and scatter on top. Serve just warm.

Serves 2

6 rashers streaky bacon

1 tablespoon olive oil

1 red onion, peeled and finely chopped

2 garlic cloves, peeled and finely chopped

2 tablespoons fresh rosemary leaves

400 g/14 oz can cooked green lentils, drained

4 tablespoons half-fat crème fraîche

1 tablespoon balsamic vinegar

60 g/2½ oz pack rocket or baby salad leaves

sea salt and freshly ground black pepper

Fig and ham plate

This is a simple antipasti-style salad and it makes a lovely, smart-looking lunch. The mixture of sweet, salty and bitter flavours all together on one plate make this really exciting to eat.

Arrange the mango, figs, ham, endive and cheese on two plates. Splash over a little oil and vinegar and serve with warmed crusty bread.

Serves 2

1 small ripe mango, peeled, stoned and sliced

3 ripe figs, quartered

4 slices of cured ham

1 head endive/chicory, separated into leaves

75 g/3 oz creamy blue cheese, such as Dolcelatte or Cambazola, diced

extra virgin olive oil and balsamic vinegar, to serve

Peppered tuna and broad bean salad

I must be the only person on the planet who isn't mad for fresh tuna, but I'm afraid I much prefer it canned, especially when you can now get such lovely fillets in spring water or good olive oil. And I don't think you can really have too much pepper, it warms the back of your throat in such a pleasing way. And yes, it's good for you, too: black pepper improves digestion and has impressive antioxidant and antibacterial effects and, best of all, the outer layer stimulates the breakdown of fat cells! Not that I've noticed.

1 Cook the beans in a pan of boiling water for 4–5 minutes until tender. If you can face it, pop the beans out of their shells – personally, I think it's worth it, the shells are quite tough and the colour of the beans within is so bright and pretty.

2 Next, empty the tuna fish into a sieve fitted over a bowl and allow it to drain, reserving the oil.

3 Using either a heavy knife or a pestle and mortar, crush the garlic with some salt to make a paste, then work the mustard powder into this. Push the mixture to one side, add the peppercorns and crush coarsely. Stir in the lemon rind and juice and 3 tablespoons of the reserved tuna oil (the rest can be discarded).

4 Arrange the rocket, tuna, onion and beans on 4 plates and drizzle over the dressing. Serve with chunks of warm crusty bread.

Serves 4

300 g/11 oz frozen broad beans

2 x 200 g/7 oz cans tuna fillets in olive oil

2 garlic cloves, peeled

1 teaspoon English mustard powder

2 teaspoons black peppercorns

grated rind and juice of 1 unwaxed lemon

50 g/2 oz rocket

1 red onion, peeled and sliced into thin rounds

flaky sea salt

Harissa'd chicken tabbouleh

Harissa is a Moroccan hot chilli sauce that's really potent. There are lots of varieties around now, but choose the coarser ones rather then the super smooth pastes as the texture is so much better. Look out too for different versions – my favourite is a rose harissa that's stocked in my local supermarket. Rub it into any chicken, meat or fish before grilling.

1 Place the bulgar in a large bowl, cover it with plenty of cold water and leave for about 20 minutes until the grains soften.

2 Meanwhile, cook the chicken under a medium grill for 8 minutes on each side until cooked through. Cut into slices.

3 In a large serving bowl, mix the harissa with the lemon juice and oil. Stir in the chicken and set aside for a few minutes until the bulgar is ready.

4 Line a colander with a clean tea towel and tip in the softened bulgar. Squeeze the cloth to get rid of as much excess water as possible. Stir into the serving bowl along with the spring onions, tomatoes, herbs, cucumber and chicken. Check the seasoning and serve.

Serves 4

300 g/11 oz bulgar wheat

2 large skinless boneless chicken breasts

1 tablespoon harissa paste

juice of 1 lemon

3 tablespoons olive oil

1 bunch of spring onions, finely chopped

4 ripe tomatoes, chopped

1 large bunch of fresh mint, chopped

1 large bunch of fresh parsley, chopped

½ cucumber, roughly chopped

sea salt and freshly ground black pepper

Goats' cheese and pomegranate couscous with pine nuts

Perfect lunchbox material. This salad keeps very well and has a great balance of flavours and textures. And pomegranates are very good for you – did you know, the ancient Egyptians were so keen on them that they included them in their tombs to ensure safe passage to the next world? Anyway, pomegranate is particularly good for the cardiovascular system and is useful for maintaining healthy blood pressure and cholesterol levels.

1 Place the couscous in a large bowl and cover with the hot stock. Set aside for 10 minutes until the grains are tender and all the liquid has been absorbed.

2 Mix the oil with the molasses and lime juice to make the dressing.

3 Using a fork, fluff up the couscous, then gently stir through the cheese, pomegranate seeds, herbs and pine nuts. Stir in the dressing and chill until ready to serve.

Serves 2

150 g/5 oz couscous

175 ml/6 fl oz hot chicken or vegetable stock

2 tablespoons extra virgin olive oil

1 tablespoon pomegranate molasses

juice of ½ lime

2 x 100 g/3½ oz slices of firm goats' cheese, crumbled

seeds of 1 pomegranate

2 tablespoons chopped fresh coriander or mint leaves

2 tablespoons toasted pine nuts

Pasta and crab salad

I love the combination of pasta and crab. Canned crab is an excellent store cupboard ingredient and as well as being very low in fat, it is high in zinc, which is good for, amongst other things, healthy sensory function, meaning it'll help you to enjoy the smell and taste of your food even more. This is lovely served hot, but is a little nicer as a room-temperature salad.

1 Cook the pasta in a pan of boiling salted water according to the packet instructions. Drain the pasta into a colander.

2 Mix the crab, lemons, oil, garlic, chilli, lemon juice, coriander leaves, a little salt and plenty of black pepper together in the hot pan. Add the drained pasta, tossing well so it is well coated in oil, herbs and crab.

3 Leave to sit for 5 minutes – it will stick together a little bit, how much depends on the type of pasta and shape you used. Eat when you're ready.

Serves 2

225 g/8 oz pasta shapes

170 g/6 oz can white crab meat, drained

2 small preserved lemons, finely chopped

3 tablespoons olive oil

1 garlic clove, peeled and crushed

1 red chilli, finely chopped

1 tablespoon fresh lemon juice

2 tablespoons chopped fresh coriander leaves

sea salt and freshly ground black pepper

Roasted halloumi and aubergine salad

I love pink peppercorns and just can't understand why they're so unfashionable. Their sweet flavour is lovely and delicate and goes very nicely with the orange I've used in the dressing. If, like everyone, you can't bear to use them either, ordinary old black peppercorns will do.

1 Preheat the oven to 200°C/400°F/mark 6. Toss together the aubergine, tomatoes, cheese and oil. Place on a shallow tray in a single layer so they roast rather than steam. Roast in the oven for 25–30 minutes until the aubergine is cooked through and nicely browned.

2 Meanwhile, to make the dressing, mix the orange rind and juice with the oil, herbs, peppercorns and some salt.

3 Tip the cooked aubergine, tomatoes and cheese into a large bowl and stir in the dressing. Leave to sit for 5 minutes.

4 Divide the baby leaves between 2 bowls and spoon the dressed warm salad on top.

Serves 2

1 large aubergine, cut into small cubes

250 g/9 oz cherry tomatoes

250 g/9 oz block of halloumi cheese, cut into small cubes

2 tablespoons olive oil

50 g/2 oz baby salad leaves

For the dressing

grated rind and juice of 1 small unwaxed orange

1 tablespoon extra virgin olive oil

1 tablespoon chopped fresh dill or tarragon leaves

1 teaspoon dried pink peppercorns, lightly crushed

sea salt

Seared beef salad with beetroot and green beans

You need a lovely piece of trimmed organic fillet of beef for this fantastic salad. It cooks best if you take it out of the fridge a good 30 minutes beforehand.

1 Cook the beans in a pan of boiling water for 4 minutes, then drain and cool.

2 Rub the beef with the oil, then roll it in the sesame seeds to coat. Cook in a hot pan for 7 minutes, turning from time to time until nicely browned. Leave to rest for 5 minutes.

3 Very thinly slice the beetroot – this is most easily done using a mandolin or other slicing machine. Separate the slices onto a platter. In a small bowl, mix the lime juice with the fish sauce, sugar and chilli. Once the sugar has dissolved, stir in the shallot, then pour the mixture over the beetroot. Set aside for 5–10 minutes.

4 Thinly slice the beef and toss with the beetroot, mint, lettuce leaves and green beans.

Serves 4

250 g/9 oz green beans

400 g/14 oz fillet of beef

1 teaspoon vegetable oil

2 teaspoons sesame seeds

2 small fresh beetroots

juice of 1 lime

2 tablespoons fish sauce

1 teaspoon caster sugar

1 small hot chilli, thinly sliced

1 shallot, peeled and thinly sliced

2 tablespoons chopped fresh mint leaves

2 little gem lettuce, leaves separated

Final Finish

Good shortbread

Okay, so if we're being healthy, we shouldn't really be eating biscuits, but we're all allowed a little bit of what we fancy once in a while and homemade is the way to go – at least you can be sure your biscuits are additive free!

Makes 35
75 g/3 oz salted butter, at room temperature

40 g/1½ oz caster sugar

40 g/1½ oz semolina

75 g/3 oz plain flour

1 Preheat the oven to 180°C/350°F/mark 4. Using electric beaters, whisk the butter and sugar together for 5 minutes until pale. With a wooden spoon, beat in the semolina and flour.

2 Roll the mixture into cherry-sized balls and place on a couple of non-stick baking sheets. Bake in the oven for 20 minutes until golden, then leave to cool.

Oat-crunch summer fruit crumble

Make this all year round using a pack of colourful, vitamin-rich, frozen summer fruits. Adding oats to a crumble is nothing new, but it just works so well! Nice warm from the oven, better cold the next day.

Serves 6
500 g/1 lb 2 oz bag frozen summer fruits, thawed

4 tablespoons blackcurrant or elderflower cordial

75 g/3 oz plain flour

75 g/3 oz plain wholemeal flour

1 teaspoon ground allspice

75 g/3 oz cold butter, diced

50 g/2 oz porridge oats

75 g/3 oz demerara sugar

1 Preheat the oven to 190°C/375°F/mark 5. Empty the fruits into a large shallow baking dish, then stir in the cordial.

2 Mix the flours with the allspice, then rub in the butter until there are no large pieces left. Stir in the oats and sugar.

3 Scatter the crumble over the fruit and bake in the oven for 40–45 minutes until nicely browned. Eat warm or cold.

Blueberry and banana puddings

People with a sweet tooth tend to enjoy proper old-fashioned steamed puddings. The problem is they are high in calories, low in nutrients and take so long to cook. This lighter version includes fresh fruit and also has a cheats' method, where individual puds can be micro-cooked in just 3 minutes!

1 Place the butter, sugar, flours, baking powder, salt and lemon rind in a large mixing bowl, then break in the eggs and whisk together, preferably with an electric hand-held whisk, until you have a soft creamy mixture.

2 Mash the bananas and stir into the mixture with the blueberries. Spoon the mixture into a 1 litre/1¾ pint buttered pudding basin and level off the surface.

3 Take a square of double thickness foil and smear it with a little butter. Make a pleat in the centre and fix it over the pudding, tying securely around the rim with string. Place the pudding in a pan, then pour in boiling water to come halfway up the side of the basin. Cover and steam for 2½ hours. Check halfway through cooking that the water in the pan isn't getting too low and top up with boiling water, if necessary.

4 Turn out and serve hot with custard.

Super-speedy version
Divide the mixture between 6 microwave-proof moulds such as teacups. Microwave on High for 2½–3 minutes until risen and firm. Leave to stand for 1 minute before serving.

Serves 8

100 g/3½ oz butter, softened, plus a little extra for greasing

100 g/3½ oz light muscovado sugar

100 g/3½ oz self-raising flour

50 g/2 oz wholemeal flour

½ teaspoon baking powder

a pinch of salt

grated rind of 1 unwaxed lemon

2 large eggs

2 ripe bananas

75 g/3 oz dried blueberries

Papaya and lime granita

Papaya is a wonder-fruit. It's low in calories but high in nutrients. It is an excellent source of beta-carotene, folate and fibre and just one half contains 150% of the recommended daily amount of vitamin C. It is also said to have healing properties, and when rubbed on to a cut will speed up the healing. And it tastes very good, too, especially when paired with lime.

1 Place the sugar, lime rind and juice, lemon grass stalk and 150 ml/¼ pint of the water in a pan. Heat gently, stirring until the sugar dissolves, then simmer gently for 5 minutes. Turn off the heat and leave to cool.

2 Meanwhile, halve the fruit, scoop out the seeds and discard. Then scoop out the flesh and whiz in a food processor until smooth.

3 Strain the lime syrup into a rigid container, then stir in the remaining water and the papaya purée. Freeze for 2 hours until almost firm, then, using a fork, break the mixture into large flaky crystals. Freeze for a further 2 hours, then break up again.

Serves 6

125 g/4 oz caster sugar

grated rind and juice of 4 unwaxed limes

1 lemon grass stalk, roughly flattened with a rolling pin

600 ml/1 pint water

2 ripe papaya

Raspberry and rosewater whips

This is incredibly simple to make but looks gorgeous. Raspberries and roses are a fantastic union.

Serves 4

250 g/9 oz fresh raspberries

50 g/2 oz caster sugar

a few drops of rosewater

250 g/9 oz fromage frais

250 g/9 oz Greek yoghurt

pink rose petals, to decorate (optional)

1 Mash the raspberries, sugar and rosewater together to a pulp.

2 In a separate bowl, whisk together the fromage frais and yoghurt, then ripple through the raspberries. Spoon into small serving glasses and chill until ready to eat. Decorate with rose petals, if you like.

Vanilla and cardamom-scented plums in port

This recipe is courtesy of my good friend and fellow food writer Jenny White. It does contain alcohol, but only one glassful for four servings and it has no added fat!

Serves 4

150 ml/¼ pint ruby port

150 ml/¼ pint water

2 tablespoons caster sugar

2 strips lemon rind

1 vanilla pod, split lengthways

1 cardamom pod, bruised

8 ripe, firm plums, halved and stoned

Greek yoghurt, to serve

1 Put the port in a saucepan with the water, sugar, lemon rind, vanilla pod and cardamom pod. Heat gently, stirring until the sugar has dissolved, then add the plums and increase the heat. Simmer for 10–15 minutes until the plums are tender but retain their shape.

2 With a slotted spoon, divide the plums between 4 serving dishes. Continue boiling the port mixture until syrupy and reduced by half. Strain the syrup and spoon over the plums. Serve warm or chilled with yoghurt.

Grape Jellies

Couldn't be easier! There are some really good-quality grape juices available now – they come in a variety of pretty colours and are naturally sweet, so all you need to do is set them.

1 Place the gelatine in a shallow dish of cold water and leave for 5 minutes until softened.

2 Heat 150 ml/¼ pint of the grape juice in a small pan until hot but not boiling. Drain the gelatine leaves and squeeze out the excess water. Add to the pan, turn off the heat and stir until dissolved, then leave to cool.

3 Add the rest of the grape juice to the gelatine mixture, then pour into 6 glasses (or plastic pots if you're planning a picnic). Scatter the blueberries on top if you have them, then cover and chill for at least a couple of hours until set.

Serves 6
5 sheets of leaf gelatine
600 ml/1 pint red grape juice
100 g/3½ oz fresh blueberries
(if you have any)

Buttermilk baked custard with orange strawberries

Buttermilk is lower in fat than regular milk since the fat has been used to make butter. It is also rich in vitamins and calcium and those who find milk difficult to digest may find buttermilk preferable as it digests more quickly. It has a gentle sour tang to it, which makes it a good substitute for yoghurt and soured cream.

1 Preheat the oven to 170°C/325°F/mark 3. In a large jug, gently whisk together the whole eggs, egg yolks, buttermilk, sugar, cornflour and vanilla extract, but not too vigorously because you don't want to make bubbles.

2 Set a deep 20–23 cm/8–9 inch round ovenproof dish on a baking sheet. Pour in the milk mixture and grate over some nutmeg. Bake in the oven for 30 minutes, until the filling is golden brown, just about firm in the centre and slightly puffed up. Be careful not to overcook as custard can develop a clotted texture that is not as nice as when it's smooth, although it will still taste good.

3 Meanwhile, place the strawberries, orange rind and juice and sugar in a shallow heatproof dish and roast alongside the custard for 15 minutes. Serve warm or chilled.

Serves 4

3 large eggs plus 2 large egg yolks

2 x 284 ml/½ pint cartons buttermilk

50 g/2 oz caster sugar

1 teaspoon cornflour

½ teaspoon vanilla extract

freshly grated nutmeg

For the strawberries

450 g/1 lb strawberries

juice and grated rind of 1 unwaxed orange

1 teaspoon caster sugar

Coffee and walnut cake

A coffee cake in such a wholesome book? Well, yes. Firstly, coffee does have its merits: a study has found it contributes more antioxidants (which have been linked with fighting heart disease and cancer) to the diet than cranberries, apples or tomatoes. And secondly, who can really be expected to live without cake once in a while?

1 Preheat the oven to 180°C/350°F/mark 4. Dissolve the coffee in the 2 tablespoons of boiling water, then set aside to cool for a while. Take out the 12 prettiest walnut halves and chop the rest.

2 Place the flour, baking powder, butter, sugar and eggs in a large bowl and whisk with electric beaters until well blended. Whisk in the cooled coffee, then stir in the chopped walnuts. Spoon the mixture into two lined non-stick 20 cm/8 inch cake tins. Bake in the oven for 30 minutes until the cakes feel a bit springy when touched.

3 Meanwhile, combine in a bowl all the ingredients for the filling.

4 For the syrup, dissolve the coffee and sugar in the boiling water. Remove the cakes from the oven. Pierce the cakes with a skewer, drizzle over the syrup and leave to cool.

5 Once cooled, sandwich the cake together with half the filling. Smooth the rest of the filling on top of the cake and decorate with the reserved walnut halves – make sure there's one on each slice. Put the kettle on!

Serves 12

4 teaspoons instant espresso coffee granules

2 tablespoons boiling water

100 g/3½ oz walnut halves

175 g/6 oz self-raising flour

1 teaspoon baking powder

175 g/6 oz butter, at room temperature

175 g/6 oz caster sugar

3 large eggs, at room temperature

For the filling

1 tablespoon instant espresso coffee powder

2 tablespoons caster sugar

250 g/9 oz Quark or other low-fat soft cheese

200 g/7 oz fromage frais

For the syrup

1 tablespoon instant espresso coffee powder

50 g/2 oz caster sugar

5 tablespoons boiling water

Iced apple mint tea

This is a fantastic summer drink. Use good-quality pressed apple juice or, for the best result, juice some Granny Smiths yourself.

Serves 2

12 fresh mint leaves

1 tea bag

400 ml/14 fl oz boiling water

200 ml/7 fl oz pressed fresh apple juice

1 green apple, sliced

ice and mint leaves, to serve

1 Place the mint and tea bag in a jug and pour over the boiling water. Leave to cool, then strain into a jug. Stir in the apple juice and chill until ready to serve.

2 Stack the sliced apple, ice and mint into 2 tall glasses and pour in the tea. Slip in straws and slurp.

Lemon barley water

Lemon drinks are very cleansing. While it's hard to knock good old-fashioned homemade lemonade, this barley water definitely has the edge over it. Try it with oranges, too.

Serves 2

50 g/2 oz pearl barley

1 litre/1¾ pints boiling water

1 small unwaxed lemon

600 ml/1 pint cold water

1 tablespoon caster sugar

1 Place the barley in a sieve and pour over the boiling water to scald and cleanse it (this aids in producing a clearer colour for the finished barley water).

2 Finely peel the lemon, trying to avoid the pith, then squeeze the juice. Place the barley, lemon rind and the cold water into a saucepan, cover and simmer gently for 20 minutes.

3 Strain the liquid through a muslin cloth into a jug, then stir in the lemon juice and sugar to taste. Allow to cool, then chill, or serve over ice.

Real ginger beer

I always find making ginger beer exciting – the fizz that builds up is amazing, which is why you must use plastic bottles since glass can explode. Ginger beer is simple to make and doesn't take much effort but you do need to plan ahead – I promise it really will be the highlight of your picnic, so it's worth the trouble. I choose regular dried yeast, not fast-acting or bread-machine yeast. Remember that because of the fermentation process this does develop a slight alcohol content.

1 Place the ginger, lemon, sugar and 500 ml/17 fl oz of the water in a large pan. Bring to the boil and simmer for 5 minutes. Pour in the remaining 1.75 litres/3 pints of water and stir in the cream of tartar and the yeast. Cover and leave overnight at room temperature.

2 Strain the liquid through a nylon sieve, then pour into clean plastic bottles, leaving a 5 cm/2 inch gap at the top. Screw on the caps and store in a cool place. Check the bottles once or twice a day – if they begin to expand outwards, unscrew the cap to allow some of the gas to escape.

3 The ginger beer should be fizzy enough in about 12 hours, but will last up to 3 days, if kept chilled – remember to keep an eye on the fizz build-up. It should taste wonderfully of ginger and lemon, so don't drink it if it's at all musty or yeasty.

Serves 8

2 tablespoons finely chopped fresh root ginger

1 unwaxed lemon, thinly sliced

250 g/9 oz caster sugar

2.25 litres/3 pints 17 fl oz cold water

½ teaspoon cream of tartar

½ x 7 g/¼ oz sachet regular dried yeast

3 x 1 litre/1¾ pint plastic bottles (or 2 x 1.5 litre/2½ pint)

Index